Ron Garland with Brian Hewitt

GOLF NUTS
You've Got To Be Committed

Foreword by Michael Jordan

Illustrations by Steve Artley

CLOCK
TOWER
PRESS

Clock Tower Press, LLC
3622 W. Liberty
Ann Arbor, MI 48103
www.clocktowerpress.com

Printed and bound in Canada.

10 9 8 7 6 5 4 3

Library of Congress Cataloging-in-Publication Data
Garland, Ronald.
Golf nuts : you've got to be committed / by Ronald Garland
with Brian Hewitt.
p. cm.
ISBN 1-58536-066-X
1. Golf-Anecdotes. I. Hewitt, Brian. II. Title.
GV967 .G25 2002
796.352—dc21
2002010783

To Judy, my wife and chief enabler

Acknowledgments

First and foremost, I would like to thank all of you golf nuts (you know who you are) who provided me with the reassurance that I wasn't alone, and with the material that made this book possible. You people are nuts.

And then a special note of thanks to the golf nut at Clock Tower Press: Golf Editor Brett Marshall — who was nuts enough to believe that a story about golf nuts would be of interest to other golf nuts.

Also a big thank you to Brian Hewitt, who did so much to make the book an easy and enjoyable read. My suspicion is that he may never recover from this little project.

Last of all, thanks to you — the reader — for being nuts enough to buy this book. I hope it brings a smile to your face. That has always been my goal since starting the Golf Nuts Society in 1986. Anyone who plays this maddening game needs a little comic relief once in a while, don't you think?

Preface

This book is not *War and Peace*. It isn't even Beyond *The Valley of the Dolls*. Arguably, it has no redeeming social value. Nor has any attempt been made in the following pages to couch any grand statements about the cosmic meaning of life. College students will never be asked to "compare and contrast" the symbolism in this book to the symbolism in William Faulkner's great short story, "The Bear."

To be sure, most golf nuts believe "The Bear" is Jack Nicklaus. Few golf nuts apologize for their priorities that often put golf ahead of almost everything else in their lives.

Tom Wolfe wouldn't buy this book on a bet. Elmore Leonard wouldn't even consider a screenplay about this material. It's safe to say John Grisham would rather pick fly droppings out of a pepper shaker than pore over this tome. But John Updike, one of the most cerebral writers of our time, might love this book if he gave it a chance. Updike, you see, is a golf nut. And golf nuts are what this book is all about.

That is not to say this is literature. No, sir. Not in the loosest sense of the definition can this be considered literature. But that doesn't mean it isn't a good read. All anybody who aspires to create something from scratch and put it on a blank page can hope to do is be good at what he or she is trying to do.

Animal House wasn't a great film in the classic sense. But it was good at what it was trying to do. Same goes for a goofy little flick called *Wayne's World*. *Caddyshack* was very good at what it was trying to do. So much so that much of its dialogue has been committed to memory by so many current touring pros that it's hard to walk down the range at a PGA Tour event and not hear daily allusions.

Caddyshack captured something all of us in golf knew existed but hadn't figured out how to express. This book about the Golf Nuts Society is a similar attempt. It is an attempt to be good at what it is trying to do. And it is an attempt to show the people who live golf to a fault that they really aren't so strange after all. The golf nuts you will read about in this book exist in the sport's twilight zone. But are they so very different in their passions for the game than you and me?

You decide. Then go back, rerent *Caddyshack* and start memorizing lines.

Go nuts
Brian Hewitt

Foreword

I first met "The Nut" (as I call him) in the summer of 1986. I was flying to Oregon a lot because of my endorsement contract with Nike, and spending a lot of time with their creative director, Peter Moore. After our meetings, Peter and I would go to his club to tee it up.

Ron "The Nut" Garland was a good friend of Peter's and was also a member there. Peter invited him to join us one day. He was the reigning Oregon Amateur Champion, and man was he competitive! Throughout the round we were having long drive contests, and closest to the pin contests, and putting contests. You name it, we did it. It was great, especially when I'd knock it by his driver with my 1-iron. He didn't enjoy that as much as I did, but what did he expect with that short quick swing of his?

On the 18th tee Peter told me about "Ron's new club." I thought he was talking about a new driver or some "super club," because Ron surely needed one. But Peter was talking about a different kind of club—something called the "Golf Nuts Society." It was a club for "golf nuts," he said. I signed up, and Ron gave me a membership kit, a couple of license plate frames for my cars, a shirt and a cap, and I was set. I was officially a Registered Golf Nut.

Over the next couple of years, whenever I found myself back in Oregon to see Nike or to play against the Portland Trailblazers, The Nut and I would tee it up and he'd ask me what I'd done to earn "Nut" points since the last time we'd played. One time we scored a ton of points ourselves when we teed off at 2:00 p.m. one afternoon and still got in 45 holes. We finished at 10:00 p.m. in total darkness. Now that was fun.

I always had some good stories, and pretty soon I'd earned enough Nut points to move into second place in the 1989 Golf Nut of the Year competition without even taking the Society's entrance exam. Now, I'm pretty competitive, and I wanted that title. So I finally took the entrance exam and "aced" it, then went on to win the 1989 Golf Nut of the Year title (there's nothing like winning). I've also been a member of the Society's Board of Directors since 1986, and for a long time I held the "All Time Leading Scorer" title too, until some other "nut" finally outscored me.

I've done some pretty crazy things to feed my golf habit, and you'll have a chance to read about some of them in this book. Like the time that I was a "no-show" for my first NBA MVP award presentation. Everybody was in Chicago for the presentation — except me. I was at Pinehurst going 36 a day with my golf buddies.

I can't think of anyone better to write about the exploits of me and the other Registered Golf Nuts than The Nut himself. He has written a very funny book about the members of his crazy society, and every story is true, which is a pretty scary thought. These guys really are nuts!

If you love golf, you'll love this book. It's for golf nuts. The certifiable kind, like you and me.

Michael Jordan
Registered Golf Nut #0023
1989 Golf Nut of the Year
Golf Nuts Society Board of Directors

P.S. And tell that "nut" who took my "All Time Leading Scorer" title that I'm coming after him.

Introduction

The Disease

Yes, golfers are nuts. I've been nuts since the first time I swung a golf club—I missed the ball completely and it made me nuts! Then, one day, I hit my first perfect shot — a "flushed" 7-iron that rose high above the trees and settled three feet from the pin. I've been nuts about the game ever since.

Golf is a love/hate relationship more complex and confusing than the battle of the sexes. If men and women fell in and out of love as fast or as often as golfers fall in and out of love with this game, there would be no such thing as love. I can't tell you how many times I've said, "I hate this game!" after a bad shot, only to be exclaiming, "I love this game!" just three swings later.

We golfers confound nongolfers. They scratch their heads in wonderment as they watch us do the most amazing and puzzling things in pursuit of a game that we say we hate. Fortunes have been spent in search of "The Secret"; lives have been risked playing in weather that has the National Weather Service issuing warnings; and marriages have been destroyed because Dad came home late for dinner—again.

It is so true that "the game will drive you nuts." I've seen it happen to so many good men and women. They live perfectly normal lives—until they get a golf club in their hands. Then they go nuts. Totally nuts. Here, see for yourself—

Doug Skille went out one summer evening to hit a few chips on a nearby green, and never returned. Well, he did finally return, but only after he had played nine holes in total darkness with only a 5-iron, a flashlight, and a couple of golf balls. It was 10:00 at night.

Steve Post played golf during his wedding rehearsal.

Jeff Larsen was practicing chip shots in his living room one evening with his favorite sand wedge when he took a carpet divot that tore through the carpet and the padding, and embedded in the plywood flooring, snapping the club shaft. Fortunately, he was able to repair the club.

Pete Schenk concluded that golf had too strong a grip on him. He needed a break, so he decided to go camping to get away from the game for a few days. But as he unpacked he discovered a sand wedge and three balls in the trunk of his car. He ended up building a makeshift nine-hole course in the woods and playing golf all weekend, right there in the campground.

Ken Hoel writes swing keys on the thumb of his golf glove, the head of his driver, and the toes of his golf shoes in a futile attempt to improve his game.

See what I mean? That's why I founded the Golf Nuts Society. These people are nuts. But golf will do that to you. Nobody really knows why, but everybody who has ever picked up a golf club will tell you that it's true. These "nuts" needed a home. We call it The Nut House. Come on in, take a seat, and enjoy a story or two about people who are probably not that much different from you.

Ron Garland
The Head Nut
Registered Golf Nut #0001

"What a wonderful way to start our honeymoon!"

1st Hole

EARLY SYMPTOMS

"During golf season he would spend every Saturday at the golf course playing, practicing, and filming his swing while the tape recorder at home was taping that week's PGA Tour event. Then he would come home and watch the taped telecast while he ate dinner, followed by video analysis of his swing until bedtime. He is truly one of a kind, and there must be something dreadfully wrong with me to have put up with it for all these years."

Judy Garland, Mrs. Head Nut

The first time I ever picked up a golf club, golf wasn't even on my mind. I was a sophomore in college and struggling to keep from getting an "F" in calculus. But my next-door neighbor just happened to be the local high school math teacher. As I walked across the lawn to beg him for help (again), he was in the front yard hitting whiffle balls with a 7-iron. "Here, hit a couple while I read the question," he said as he took my calculus book from me.

I took a swing, and smacked that whiffle ball clear across the yard. "Wow! You're a natural!" he observed. "You should take up the game." But all I wanted to do at the time was pass calculus, which I did. Barely. I got a "D".

I didn't know it at the time, but I was in the presence of my first "golf nut." I wish I could remember his name, but what I do remember is that he would hit balls into the field behind his house almost every evening. Then once a week or so, he'd wander aimlessly about in that field and try to find some of the balls he had hit. He didn't find very many because the weeds were waist high. That was "nuts." But it's nothing compared to some of the things I've done and seen since.

It was about a year later that I had my second encounter with golf. By this time I had migrated north to Humboldt State (CA) University for my final two years of college (it ended up being three, but who's counting). One of my college roommates asked me if I wanted to join them for a round of golf at Eureka Muni, the local goat track. And for some unexplained reason I said, "Yes." There have been times over these past 30-plus years when I wished I'd said "No!" But I didn't, and now I'm writing a book about my addiction. Oh well, maybe it'll be therapeutic.

About the only thing I knew about golf the first time I teed it up was that I didn't have any clubs, and that you wore wingtips when you played. No problem on the wingtips. I played in my black dress shoes and a cool Hogan cap even though I didn't know who Hogan was. I borrowed a few clubs from one of my other roommates who apparently didn't want to have anything to do with playing golf with a rank beginner. As it turned out, he was clairvoyant. I shot 160, while breaking at least one USGA rule, and losing at least one ball, on every hole. So much for being a "natural."

When I started the round there were six golf balls in my roommate's bag. When I finished the round there were seven, which included none of the original six! Needless to say, I spent a lot of time in the bushes. But it was fun. I still remember that day fondly more than 30 years later. I guess you could say it was the beginning of the end of life as I knew it.

After that early baptism at Eureka Muni, my roommates and I tried to play once a week, mostly at my prodding. I was hooked, and I didn't have a car. Speaking of beginners, here is one of my favorite Nut stories along those lines:

Ken Huckins, Registered Golf Nut #0409, spent over $3,000 on golf equipment in his first two months as a golfer. Now that's a serious commitment. And it didn't even include the money he spent on green fees, range balls, instruction books, or lessons. I gave him 1,300 Nut points for that one (Don't worry, we'll talk about Nut points a little later). In one round of golf he lost 25 golf balls. He even had to return to the pro shop three times to buy more ammo just to finish the round. He finally finished in total darkness with a ball from a playing companion. That little episode got him another 250 points.

In my final year of college I married Judy Brown, making her an instant celebrity (Judy Garland). I'll never forget that moment when I proposed to her. After she accepted, I had this terrible, sinking feeling. I thought, "What if she doesn't want me to play golf?" I quickly gathered myself for the moment of truth and said, "Now, Judy, you need to know something. I loved golf before I loved you; don't ever make me choose." And to this day she's never called my bluff. Some guys are just lucky, I guess. We've been married 31 years.

As for the ultimatum? Judy has her own version. "It's kind of like one of those urban legends," she says. "I don't remember those actual words being said. But you knew you didn't dare cross him when it came to golf. He basically played golf every weekend and almost every afternoon for the first 29 years of our marriage. But if he were around all the time at home, he'd be underfoot. It makes for a better marriage if you have less time to argue. I've enjoyed tremendous freedom.

"Golf is Ron's passion. There would be no way to stop it even if I wanted to. A lot of people don't know that originally Ron was going to be a forest ranger. He would have been a triple Type A forest ranger. Now he actually plays golf a little less than he used to. He's a major entrepreneur. With the Golf Nuts Society he's got a million things going at all times. If Ron had married another woman, she probably would have killed him by now or he would have been divorced 50 times. I have other interests from golf."

God bless Judy.

The first test of our relationship came when I found out that the local country club had a special deal for college students. For only a $60 initiation fee and monthly dues of $18, I could become a proud member of Baywood Golf & Country Club. It was a great track, once hosting the legendary Ben Hogan for an exhibition round when he was in his prime. What a deal.

Now, a college student doesn't make much money, especially a newlywed. In my case, I wasn't making any money, since I was a full-time student. Judy had dropped out after her junior year to support us while I got my degree. She worked at a local clothing store. Needless to say, this was going to be a very delicate negotiation. But faced with such a great deal, how could any clear-thinking golf nut not join the club?

Judy agreed to fund this first of many golf boondoggles, and I was accepted as a member of Baywood Golf & Country Club. One small problem: We only had one car. Easy solution. We rented a house just a mile from the course. After classes (ahem, and after I finished studying) I would walk to the golf course if Judy was working. Faced with the prospect of walking home after my round, I found a better arrangement. I just stayed at the golf course until Judy got off work, at which time she would come pick me up.

This arrangement slowly evolved into, "Hey Judy, why don't you just relax for a while when you get home, and then come get me when it gets dark." She agreed, and would show up in the parking lot just before dark. Most of the time I would be on the putting green, and just jump in the car for the short ride home. But then one evening I was having a little difficulty with my putting about the time Judy pulled into the lot. I just happened to notice that it wouldn't be all that hard for her to drive the car up beside the practice putting green and, if she parked it just right...Well, you get the idea. I putted pretty darn well that night, and Judy didn't divorce me. Which is nice.

"No way on earth I'd put up with that again," Judy says now. "He'd say, 'just one more putt.' And I'd sit there like..........a young wife."

Thirty-one years later I don't think I'd try that one again. Besides, I do my evening putting practice in the house now mainly because I had a say in choosing the carpet. Berber, stimped out at around eleven. Rolls real nice. Judy got to pick the color. I like to encourage a team environment whenever possible.

Judy Garland: "I guess I fell in love with Ron because he was cute. But he also had better values than a lot of guys. Interestingly, our daughter Kristin hates golf. But she loves her dad. When it comes to the golf we kind of make faces behind his back a lot. Ron doesn't get a lot of sleep. And he gets migraines. But everything he does, he does 500 per cent. At one point he wanted to be a basketball coach. He was going to be the next John Wooden."

Baywood was a wonderful golf playground. There wasn't a whole lot of play, even on the weekends. So I got my $18 worth every month. The course was closed Mondays, but that didn't stop me. I just sneaked on and played until the green superintendent chased me off.

My earliest and fondest memories of Baywood were those times when I played by myself, hitting a couple of balls on each hole as I explored the mysterious world of swing theory. Just my clubs, my 3 x 5 cards, and me. Haven't I told you about the 3 x 5 cards? Let's just say that I'm a perfectionist. Like any new-to-the-game "nut," I devoured the golf instruction magazines. I read—and believed—every word they wrote. It wasn't until years later that I discovered they contradicted what they wrote every three months or so—just so they wouldn't run out of stuff to write.

My 3 x 5 card was my constant companion on the course. At first, I'd write down just one swing thought, and pull the 3 x 5 card out of my hip pocket whenever I forgot what I had written down. But after a few days of reading, I had filled up the entire front of the card with swing keys. I had to stop to read it before every swing. Soon I discovered there was an entire backside of the card upon which I could write. Then I graduated to 4 x 6 cards. There was so much to remember. It got so bad that I would read both sides of the card before every shot.

After a few months of this madness, I threw away the 4 x 6 cards, and started playing by feel. Of course, my definition of "feel" was how many swing thoughts I could remember while I was swinging. As I recall, it wasn't very many before my brain would melt and I'd hit a big looper to the left of left.

Which reminds me of one of my favorite Nuts: Ernest Vandeweghe Sr., Nut #1191. Ernest was named 1993 Golf Nut of the Year, and boy did he earn the title! He was the proud owner of virtually every golf instruction video ever produced since the 1940s. Talk about confusion. He had two VCRs in his home: one for watching instruction videos, and one for taping golf tournaments. He picked up a tidy 550 points for that bit of insanity.

After college I moved to Vancouver, WA, near Portland, OR, with every intention of putting my five-year teaching degree to good use. But upon arriving in town I heard through the golf grapevine that there was an opening at Royal Oaks Country Club for an assistant pro. Now, to put things in perspective, I was totally hooked on golf, and this was a golf course that had just made *Golf Digest*'s first Top 100 list (#48 to be exact.) And I had the opportunity to work there? At minimum wage? It was a no-brainer.

Of course, there was the small matter of my not being a professional. But I could apply after I started working. I took the job, and my wife was now convinced I was completely nuts. She also wondered why she had even bothered to help me get my degree. "A minimum wage job? Is this guy even capable of rational thought?"

The job lasted exactly six weeks. A four-week golf career, followed by my two-week notice. I quit. I never did apply to become a professional. Why didn't somebody tell me golf pros don't get to play golf? It was horrible. I felt like the proverbial cat staring into the fish tank. Everyone around me was playing golf while I looked out of the pro shop window at them. I became a teacher—at least for a while.

Speaking of golf professionals, it reminds me of one of the more bizarre periods in my life. Back in the early 1980s, when amateur phenom Bobby Clampett splashed upon the professional golf scene, I decided that *The Golfing Machine*, written by the late Homer Kelley, was "The Secret." You may recall Clampett was a student of Ben Doyle, who was a disciple of Homer Kelley and his book, *The Golfing Machine*. In retrospect, it is undoubtedly the most difficult book I have ever read, but that didn't deter me. I bought a copy of the book as soon as I could get my hands on one, and read it cover to cover in about two hours.

Not long after that, I had to drive five hours to Spokane, WA for the Spokane Open. So I read it again—while I drove. After the tournament, which wasn't particularly fruitful for me, I read it again on the drive home. I've never been accused of being normal, and this incident didn't do much to change my reputation.

Still not satisfied, and even more confused than before, I decided to fly to California to take lessons from Doyle himself. Over the next year and a half I flew to Carmel Valley to meet with him several times, taking five or six lessons during that time. One of them was a nine-hole playing lesson.

Not wanting to forget anything, I also filmed the lessons. I even flew to Denver to watch Bobby play in the Colorado Open and had lunch with him after filming his swing on the driving range.

But back to Ben. He had me standing on a milk crate swinging a mop while my camera recorded it for posterity. I wasn't above making a fool of myself if it meant that I might discover "The Secret." And boy, did I feel foolish. I must have looked pretty foolish, too, because everyone on the range stopped hitting balls and watched me. I think they wanted to see if I was going to fall off the milk crate. I even saw a couple of guys making bets at the end of the range.

Still obsessed with the idea that I was as close as I would ever be to "The

Secret," I tracked down the author himself· Homer Kelley. He was living in Seattle, only three hours from my home. I called him and told him that I had filmed Bobby's swing (he had never met Clampett), and that I would like to show it to him. He enthusiastically agreed, and invited me to visit him at his home.

When I arrived I was pleasantly surprised to meet Bruce Hough, Homer's top disciple, and the three of us visited for hours as we watched the video and discussed swing theory (Homer concluded that Bobby was a "hitter," not a "swinger" of the club). It was a great day. Bruce and I became friends, and would get together from time to time to hit balls and discuss the swing. It was the best of times, but it wasn't "The Secret." It was, however, the closest I had ever come to discovering it.

The real thing would come many years later. If I had known then that it would take another 20 years to discover "The Secret," I would have taken up fly-fishing much sooner and quit this maddening game for good. Another great book that purportedly held "The Secret" within its pages was *Golf in the Kingdom*. When it first came out, everyone was reading it. I even proclaimed it the "official book of the Golf Nuts Society," right up there with *Caddyshack* as the "official movie of the Golf Nuts Society." The movie survived, but the book didn't. I read it three times and couldn't find "The Secret" anywhere in it, so it was replaced with *Missing Links*, clearly the funniest and greatest golf book ever written. *Missing Links* didn't hold "The Secret" either, but it was funnier. Call it an arbitrary ruling on my part. I can take the heat.

Magazines were a big part of my early search for "The Secret." At one time I subscribed to nine different golf publications, and read every one of them cover to cover. Now that I've discovered "The Secret," I'm down to just three. However, just in case what I have discovered turns out not to be "The Secret," I've had the foresight to have saved every single issue of *Golf* Magazine and *Golf Digest* since 1969. I have several years' worth of *Golf World* and *Golfweek* magazines, too.

That's well over 600 magazines. But you can't ever be too careful when stalking "The Secret." It has a way of changing without notice, usually in the middle of your greatest round in history.

My search for "The Secret" made me do some pretty strange things in those early years, not that I've changed all that much. I was one of the first golfers to film my swing, and back then it was 8mm reels. You had to film your swing and take the reel to the camera shop, where they would send it out for processing. About a week later the film would arrive and I would put up the screen in the living room, fire up the projector and watch my swing (the only problem was that I had usually made about four swing changes by the time the film got back). There was no slow motion play-back either. One speed: fast. You had to film in slow motion if you wanted to see your swing in slow motion. And forget about stop-action. It didn't exist, unless the projector got stuck and burned a hole in your film.

Even though technology has changed a lot, I guess I haven't much. As I write this, there is a digital video camera in the trunk of my car with my clubs.

My early symptoms were easy to spot. When you hit drives down the first fairway of your golf course in the gathering darkness because there's no driving range, that's pretty nuts. I used to do that three or four times a week. I lost a lot of balls, and the green superintendent wasn't too happy either, but I had to practice somewhere. And boy, did I practice!

My passionate pursuit of "The Secret" in the early days of my budding golf career didn't border on obsession. It was more like a deep, untreatable psychosis. On the weekends when there wasn't a tournament I would play 18 holes in the morning and practice all afternoon—right up until dinner, which was at 7:30 p.m. Dinner was at 7:30 because we finally had to set a firm time for me. Otherwise, there was no telling what time I would get home. Even after we set a "curfew" for me, there were dozens of times when I would call from the pro shop to say that I was "just leaving," and of course it was after 7:30.

When there was a tournament I would be at the course before or after the round, practicing. I might as well have been a touring pro. I was a victim of my own obsessive-compulsive behavior, and I had found the perfect medium for self-discovery and self-flagellation: golf. The never-ending search for perfection.

While I was at the course, playing and practicing—or playing in a tournament—the video recorder was busily taping that weekend's PGA Tour event. I would come home, eat dinner, rewind the tape, and watch the golf tournament. Sometimes after dinner I would go to the local driving range to "hit a quick bucket because my swing was a mess and I had a tournament the next weekend." It's a wonder I'm still married.

So those were the early days. A solid foundation upon which to build "the most unique golf association in the world": The Golf Nuts Society. Thankfully, most of the members understand me.

"Ron Garland is an absolute hi-tech nut," said Joe Malay, the first Golf Nut of the Year. "He's wound up tighter than the band on a watch and he can explode at any time. But he doesn't do any damage when he explodes. He has a lovely family and wife."

"Honey, look at my score!"

2nd Hole

THE NUTS GET ORGANIZED

"Ron Garland was once voted by my little design office as the "WORST CLIENT OF THE YEAR." Talk about anal. In one meeting I described him as "visually illiterate"..............it went on and on..........knew what he wanted but hadn't seen it yet...........worried countless hours about the 'walnut' vs. another type of nut, etc. If he wasn't a friend and a golf buddy, I would have thrown him out of the office long ago. However, he is the very best sales guy I have ever known.........tried once to hire him for Nike who at that time had no clue about sales."
—**Peter Moore, Golf Nut and former Nike creative director**

"Garland, you're nuts!" I heard that a lot. Not that it was all that unfamiliar to anyone. The term "golf nut" has always been used to describe those who are terminally screwed up by the game. But nobody had ever been nuts enough to organize the troops until I decided to volunteer for the job.

Actually, my motive was a selfish one. I really, really, really needed to be reassured that I wasn't alone; that there were people out there who were just as nuts as me. Sixteen years later, I can happily report that there are plenty of people out there who are just as screwed up as me. I feel very reassured.

My wife, however, still doesn't think I'm "normal."

"Hey Judy, listen to this one. This guy's every bit as nuts as me."

"Okaaayyy....," she would say in that bored-as-hell way of hers, which was her way of saying, "So, what's your point?"

"Well, I don't know. How about that perhaps I'm not abnormal?"

"I don't think so."

But at least now I have a legion of fellow golf nuts that don't see anything wrong with the things I do. There is security in numbers, I guess.

Judy's take on this: "Somebody in the family has to have their feet on the ground." I don't think she's referring to me.

In putting this small band of rebels together, it was pretty obvious that certain people were more nuts than others. So I designed an entrance exam that would help find out just how nuts they were. The exam was divided into three sections: Commitment, Attitude, and Mechanics.

The Commitment section deals with questions about behavior. Things like, "How many times have you been threatened with divorce over golf?" Or, "How many times have you played golf in a snowstorm?" You know, the standard stuff.

The Attitude section of the exam asks the golfer to answer questions like, "When I say, 'Give me one more shot, I don't mean whiskey (True or False.)" We also ask how many golf magazines you subscribe to; a very good sign of a nut having "the right stuff."

The Mechanics section is where we find out how many times you've changed your swing, how many new clubs you've bought, and how many times you've discovered "The Secret." Of course, the more times, the better. It would be very abnormal if it was only once.

Once the exam was finished, I turned my attention to a logo. Any self-respecting golf society needs a bag tag, and to have a bag tag, I needed a logo. So I came up with the idea of a walnut on a tee, and asked fellow golf nut Peter Moore to design it for me. In return for his services, I promised to make him Nut #0002. I thought it was a fair trade. especially considering that Peter was the creative director of Nike at the time, and the man responsible for creating the "Air Jordan" logo for the great Michael Jordan. I mean, think about it. How many guys get to be Nut #0002? That's right—one. Fair trade.

After the bag tag, my focus became the membership card. I wanted to make membership in our society—as well as our membership card—extra special. So first I gave everyone a Nut # (I'm Nut #0001, for example.) But we still needed a motto; something special. Something that would say who and what we are. And since each member is known as a "Registered Golf Nut" (i.e., Peter Moore, Registered Golf Nut #0002), the motto was actually pretty easy. Here it is:

"If You're Not Registered, How Can You Be Committed?"

Now isn't that just perfect? Nothing says who we are better than that!

"Hey, but what about certified golf nut?" you ask. Answer: you have to earn that designation. When a Registered Golf Nut has earned 10,000 Nut points, he or she will earn the designation, Certified Golf Nut, and will receive a free certificate from the Society commemorating the occasion. It's one thing to be "nuts," it's another thing to be certified.

A new member receives a membership kit that includes a bag tag, a membership card, the infamous entrance exam, and a welcome letter that introduces them to our unique culture. And this is a good time to talk about our culture, which can be summed up in three words: humor, recognition, and competition.

The humor comes from the zany antics of our members. It's been said that in order for comedy to be funny, it has to be believable and based in reality. Well, let me tell you that after leading these Nuts into battle over the past sixteen years, I can comfortably report to you that their stories are both unbelievable and unreal and every last one of them is absolutely true. They're also some of the funniest stories, in my opinion, that I've ever read; which, by the way, is the best part of my job. Everyday, I get to read the letters and E-mails from these Nuts, and it makes my day. So, I decided to share the stories with the entire membership.

The members receive a daily E-mail that's very short, and very funny in a nutty kind of way. The E-mails are the foundation of our culture. They "recognize" the bizarre behavior that defines us. Think of them as a golf nut's daily "golf fix." Categories like: Nut Case of the Week; Golf Nut Record Book; The Nut Gallery, etc. All starring a cast of thousands of golf nuts. It's priceless nut stuff, and just what a golf nut needs to start his day. For example:

Hey Nut Cases,
Here's this week's Nut Case of the Week...
Shaughn Belmore (Nut #0504) - Shattered a ceiling light, poked a hole in the ceiling, took a carpet divot, and wiped out a table lamp with a single swing in his mother's living room. 400 points
Go Nuts!
The Head Nut #0001

That's the kind of stuff our members get every day. It's fun, it's short, and it's true. You might have noticed that Shaughn Belmore earned 400 points for his memorable practice swing, which is another cornerstone of the Society: earning points for lunatic behavior. Points are earned in a couple of ways: first, by taking the entrance exam, a Nut can earn several thousand points [the current record is 18,813 points by Ken Stankiewicz, (Nut #2858)].

"I knew I had found the right society the minute I read the entrance exam," said Scott Masingill, perhaps the best player in the society and a member of the Idaho Hall of Fame. "All of the things that I was thinking that bordered on insanity were down in black and white. I felt like someone had gotten into the recesses of my brain and picked out the information. I was hooked on the society at that moment."

But we don't want to limit our members' abilities to "score," so we let them turn in bonus points petitions for anything they've done that falls outside the boundaries of the entrance exam. That's when it really gets interesting.

As you can see from the story about Shaughn Belmore, he received a little "recognition," and a few points. If he keeps up the good work, he might even be named Golf Nut of the Month one day. As a Registered Golf Nut, he's also automatically entered into the Golf Nut of the Year derby. This is simply the most unique competition in golf. If he keeps accumulating Nut points, he could eventually be named Golf Nut of the Year—golf's most prestigious title.

Once he or she has won the Golf Nut of the Year (GNOTY) title, a Nut can't win it again, because certain people are just inherently more "nuts" than others. However, they can chase the title of "All-Time Leading Scorer." The way this competition works is that the Nut retains all of his Nut points. He can update his exam score annually, and can continue to accumulate points for the rest of his or her obsessive-compulsive life. The All-Time Leading Scorer is the Nut with the most points at the end of each year, which is the same as the Golf Nut of the Year competition. He or she is just not eligible for the GNOTY title anymore. Former GNOTYs have their own special place on our Web site, just as the Golf Nut of the Year does.

The Web site (www.golfnuts.com) is the focal point of our society; the online headquarters, so to speak. The USGA has their "Golf House," and we have our "Nut House." It is the central repository for some of the most unbelievable golf stories you will ever read. It's where you can see great photos of golf nuts at play. It's where you go to see who is leading the current year's Golf Nut of the Year competition (we call it The Golf Nut Tour,) and where you can read about past golf nut greats.

The future also looks very bright for the Society. With plans for Golf Nut Getaways to major championships, and exotic places like St. Andrews, Pebble Beach, Bandon Dunes, World Golf Village, and just about any other place that a golf nut would want to visit, it is our goal to "overdose" on this wonderful game as often as possible.

Golf Nut Golf Schools are also in the planning stages so that we all can eventually discover that elusive "Secret," and there will one day be a climactic Golf Nuts Championship, where we will announce the Golf Nut of the Year in front of thousands of screaming Nuts.

So there you have it: humor, recognition, and competition. Our culture. In a word: "fun." After all, isn't that what golf is supposed to be (except after a three-putt, O.B., shank, chunk, skull or water ball)?

3rd Hole

NUT BOWL I

Football has its Super Bowl; the golf nuts have the Nut Bowl. It's not actually called the Nut Bowl, but it is the Super Bowl of golf tournaments. When the Nuts have a tournament, they have a good time.

And in keeping with the theme of "humor, recognition, competition," I decided it was time to test the culture at the grassroots level. Living in the Pacific Northwest at the time, and having a pretty large number of members in the area, I scheduled Nut Bowl I: The Western Regional Golf Nuts Championship. It was 1989, the Nuts responded, and the games began. As if by destiny, it absolutely poured all day. Buckets of rain. And it was an 18-hole stroke play event.

While we do take shooting a good score seriously, we try not to take ourselves too seriously at these events. We have the typical low gross and low net prizes, but we like to make sure that those who spend their golf careers struggling in anonymity are also recognized. We do it with prize categories like Most Water Balls, Fewest Greens, Most Logos, Best Dressed, Worst Hole, Worst Swing, Farthest From The Hole But Still On The Green…well, you get the idea. We have fun.

As I mentioned, we don't take ourselves too seriously, but we understand there are those of us who are serious about posting the best score possible. The competition at our events covers all aspects of the game, including low gross and low net. We just happen to think there's more to this game than posting a score. Let me describe a few of the things that happened at Nut Bowl I. I think you'll get the idea.

At the awards dinner, we began the proceedings by discussing a few business issues that had come up after the invitations had been sent. There were certain Nuts who couldn't make the event for a variety of reasons, and these cases were brought before the membership at large for disciplinary action. Here are the pertinent cites from the minutes of that meeting:

Paul Garneau (#0312): Was attending his 35-year college class reunion at the West Point Military Academy. Recommended Action: 90 days probation; reinstatement by unanimous vote of the board of directors. Action of the Membership: Loud applause, taken as a sign of complete agreement with the recommendation.

Marty Price (#0038): Was attending the Council of Logistics Management Conference in St. Louis. Recommended Action: 30 days probation, with automatic reinstatement after 30 days. Action of the Membership: None opposed.

Bob Wiswall (#0876): Went duck hunting, but promised to take his pitching wedge and hit practice shots from the duck blind whenever there was a break in the action. Recommended Action: Letter of reprimand. Action of the Membership: Loud applause.

Bob Herb (#0300) and Gail Pugh (#0301): Went to a Washington Huskies football game. Recommended Action: 60 days probation. Reinstatement by unanimous vote of the board of directors. Action of the Membership: Grudging agreement (a couple of Oregon Ducks alumni recommended stronger measures, but we didn't have a rope).

Doug Banks (#1086): Went to a baby shower with his wife. Recommended Action: Indefinite suspension. Reinstatement at the whim of The Head Nut (That's me). Action of the Membership: A near riot broke out, and strong language was heard from every corner of the room.

Order was restored, and the membership reluctantly agreed to the recommendations of The Head Nut.

After the disciplinary actions were voted on, we moved on to less divisive issues. Dignitaries were introduced. They included: Board Members: Peter "Logo Man" Moore; Don "The Prez" Rose, the president of the Golf Nuts Society, and the man in charge of (someday) discovering "The Secret," Joe Malay, the first-ever Golf Nut of the Year.

Hall of Famers included: Robert "Bobby" Ball, the first man in GNS history to achieve the Golf Nut Slam by playing golf on New Year's Day, Easter, Mother's Day, Thanksgiving, and Christmas in a single year; Jim Gibbons, featured in a *Golf* Magazine article for playing in a golf tournament under an assumed name to keep from getting caught by his boss.

Celebrities: Ronald Reagan: it was actually Gregg "The Dalai Lama" Guernsey wearing a Ronald Reagan mask, but the crowd went wild with applause anyway. He looked like a celebrity to them.

Guernsey, in true nut fashion, remembers the Reagan mask and the event, but not the name "Nut Bowl."

"There were all kinds of characters and lots of postround antics back at Garland's house," says Guernsey now. "As you know, golfers love to tell stories......especially among themselves. And this was the mother lode gathering of storytellers. When I stepped up to the first tee wearing the Reagan mask I can remember Ron saying something like: 'Now, on the first tee, playing out of his ranch in Southern California, Ronald Reagan.' I walked slowly and I shook my head to the side like our former President was apt to do. But with the mask on I was disoriented and unbalanced and only hit it 50 yards or so. The guys circled around the tee buckled over in laughter.

"I can remember wild outfits, crazy looking clubs, goofy hats, but most of all the story telling. Joe Malay from Idaho had the craziest outfit and a driver that he pumped up with air."

"Nut Bowl was like going to the prom without a date," Malay says.

"Everybody was wondering what these other nuts would look like. When you sit down and talk to any nut, you find out the game has driven them to where they've gotten. They were good people at Nut Bowl I. My clothes were so loud they heard me before I got there."

But, Guernsey added, "I am sorry, I don't know what the Nut Bowl is." He just didn't remember the name. Zero points.

Neither did Steve Thorwald (#0476), who was also there. "But then, what can I say?" he said. "I'm a Super Senior and the mind is the second— or is it the third—thing to go."

Meanwhile, some of the auction items were pretty great too. Jack Lemmon (yes, the actor) (#0820) donated a crystal-headed, graphite-shafted putter engraved with Lemmon's autograph. Michael Jordan (#0023) donated a sleeve of personalized "MJ" Titleist golf balls, and autographed a Golf Nuts Society sweatshirt and golf cap. Bob Hope sent us a personally autographed Chrysler Classic golf cap. Awesome stuff, and a handful of lucky Nuts took them home that evening.

We wrapped up the first-ever Golf Nuts Society event with the awarding of the prizes, and the introduction of some of the more "committed" attendees.

They included: Steve Post (#0623) who played golf during his wedding rehearsal. (Talk about an early warning shot over the bow of that marriage!)500 points.

Forest Beaudry (#0390): Wore golf shoes to his wedding; and then, on the first day of his honeymoon left his wife in the car and went out to play "a quick four holes" by himself in a driving rainstorm. While on the four-hole loop, he ran into his new bride's father, brother, and brother-in-law, and wound up playing 18 holes, returning to the car four hours later. 500 points.

Johnny Curtis (#0573) Had recently undergone neck surgery, but against doctor's orders, the moment he returned home he began practicing putting throughout the house. A few days later, he was chipping in the backyard, and within a week, he was on the driving range hitting balls, again in violation of doctor's instructions. 800 points.

Steve Thorwald (#0476): Played golf on his wedding day with his future father-in-law. They changed into tuxedos at the golf course, without a shower (they were running late). They barely made the ceremony. Then, as if to test the marriage even further, on the first morning of his honeymoon he teed-off at 7:32 a.m. and played 36 holes, followed by yet another 36 holes on each of the next three days. 1,688 points.

Walt Chambers (#0285): He has six children, the youngest three of which were born while he was on the golf course. However, he reminds us proudly, he wasn't a golfer until after the third child was born. 2,000 points.

Thaddeus Czerniak (#1027): I read the following short letter I had received from #1027, which brought the house down. "I haven't been home since July 6th (it was October). To tell the truth, I think I'm divorced. However, there are some great courses in California and Nevada."500 points.

Mike Bourne (#0793): Bought a $20,000 motor home for the family, but on one condition: it doesn't leave the driveway unless he has a tee time at a golf course near their destination. 300 points.

John Day (#0402): Had recently driven 1,200 miles carrying his golf clubs in the toilet of his minimotor home. Sadly, he was only able to get them out twice during the trip to play golf. But he did visit Golf House, the home of the USGA, while on the trip. 250 points.

Dwane Brands (#0786): In August of 1932 he climbed Mt. Hood with a 5-iron strapped to his back, and upon reaching the summit, he sent a ball sailing down the north slope. 500 points.

Mike Brands (#0774): Was arrested and charged with attempted manslaughter for hitting golf balls off the south rim of the Grand Canyon. He plea-bargained, pleading guilty to the reduced charge of littering, and paid the $10 fine. (He's Dwane's son. It must be hereditary.) 1,000 points.

Dr. Jeff Leinassar (#0009): Has a putting cup embedded in the floor of the waiting room in his dental office. Putters and golf balls stand nearby just in case a patient wants to hit a few putts while they wait. 500 points.

Jeff Larsen (#0467): Was practicing the art of pinching the ball in the living room of his home when he got a little carried away and took a carpet divot that tore through the carpet and the padding and embedded in the plywood flooring, snapping the shaft of his favorite sand wedge. Fortunately, he was able to repair the sand wedge. 500 points.

Bob Miller (#0677): While practicing chip shots with a 7-iron in the hallway of his home, he "got hold of one," sending a beautiful screamer right through his daughter's bedroom window. She was grounded at the time for breaking the very same window a week earlier. 500 points.

Marshall Gleason (#0008): Took a crowbar to the trunk of his rental car while on vacation because he had accidentally locked the clubs in the trunk while standing in the parking lot of the golf course, about to tee off. The golf course was Pinehurst, and he did make his tee time. 500 points.

Jim Neilsen (#0859): During one round, his 3-iron broke, impaling his left bicep. He took off his t-shirt and wrapped it around the wound to stop the bleeding, and finished the round. 1,200 points.

These "totally committed" luminaries brought the house down, and still remain in the hearts and minds of their fellow nuts to this day. As the crowd dispersed, more than one individual was overheard saying, "Those guys are nuts."

Yes, they are.

And so ended Nut Bowl I.

"People don't understand how you can sit down with another Golf Nut and talk trash and accomplish absolutely nothing. Golf brought us together. The toughest thing about golf is not talking about it."

"A lot," says Peter Moore today, "has passed by since then."

"I'll show 'em who's boss!"

4th Hole

THE PREZ

When I founded the Golf Nuts Society, I decided I needed a president. This person would report directly to me, and his job would be to discover "The Secret." It would have to be someone consumed by golf, someone who was not afraid to change his swing, or try new equipment. It would have to be someone who didn't let small distractions such as family or career get in the way of his pursuit of "The Secret." I knew instinctively that there was only one man for the job: Don Rose. We just knew him as "Rosy."

"Rosy? You mean that tall, white-haired guy with the wet towel hanging off the back of his pants? The goofy guy with the goofy pull cart with bicycle wheels? The guy with the 'chicken wing' follow-through?"

Sure, everybody knows a guy like Rosy. Isn't he the guy who changes his swing every other day?

So it was that I named Rosy the president of the Golf Nuts Society. Recognizing that "Mr. President" was far too formal a title for such a weird guy, I shortened his title to "The Prez," which was more in keeping with his personality. "Surely, he would discover 'The Secret,'" I thought. Well, so far he hasn't, but he keeps searching. It's his job.

The Prez is one of the most unforgettable individuals I've ever met. Nobody I know can change their swing more often, with less positive effect, than The Prez. When he's running a little late for a tee time, he can change from business suit to golf clothes while speeding along the freeway at breakneck speeds. He has taken lessons from every teaching pro in the entire state of Oregon. "Now how do you know that?" you ask? Well, a few years ago, at an Oregon PGA annual meeting, the speaker asked all of the pros in the room to raise their hands if they had given Don Rose a golf lesson. All but two of them raised their hands, and those two had just moved to the state a few weeks earlier. Sadly, his swing still looks the same as it did 30 years ago.

Rosy goes to the local golf superstore (Fiddler's Green) virtually every day. He's on a first-name basis with everyone who works there. When a new instruction video shows up, he doesn't buy it; he "previews" it on the television at the store. Only then does he decide if he should buy it.

My favorite story about The Prez is the time he three-putted the 12th green at his home course, Eugene Country Club. He responded by running off the green screaming at the top of his lungs and jumping into the lake next to the green. When he came up for air, he was covered in duck poo from head to toe, but walked directly to the 13th tee and finished the round. Needless to say, the rest of his foursome walked up the opposite side of every fairway all the way to the clubhouse.

Rosy's passion for the game is legendary, and it was amply demonstrated when he decided to get married a second time (the first marriage ended when he decided to practice chipping when his first wife told him they needed to talk about how much golf he played). His new bride, Debbie, knew he played golf, but did not know the depth of his affliction. So when Debbie agreed to go to Pebble Beach for their honeymoon, she had no idea what she was about to experience.

I'll let Debbie take it from here and allow her to add a few humorous post-honeymoon anecdotes:

THE HONEYMOON: "Don says to me, 'Honey, I have the perfect place for our honeymoon: Pebble Beach.' Sounded good to me. The first morning we wake up and roll over and look into each other's eyes and he says to me, 'Honey, would it be all right if I go out and play golf today?' I blissfully respond, 'Yes, you darling, go right ahead.' The next morning we wake up and roll over and look into each other's eyes and he says to me, 'Honey, could I go out and play golf again today?' I think to myself, okay, let him get it out of his system. The third morning I wake up and roll over and he is gone! I had a difficult time deciding who to call: My mother, my attorney, or a counselor. He talked me into the counselor. That's another story. We're celebrating our 20th anniversary of marriage June 5th (2002), thank you very much."

THE CREDIT CARD: "Don announces to me one day that I am spending far too much at Nordstrom's and that I will need to cut back. That afternoon while he was playing golf I researched the budget book, credit card receipts, and check registers. When he came home and I showed him what he had spent that year on golf, he said to me, 'Honey, you just go right ahead and spend whatever you want.' The subject never came up again."

THE BIG WHITE LIE: When it came time to travel north to Washington for my family reunion, my dear husband came down with a terrible cold and explained he couldn't possibly join me on the trip. I called him each night to see how he was doing and he sounded worse each day, but by the time I returned home Sunday evening he seemed pretty good. His best friend called that evening and asked how 'Rosy' did in the golf tournament that weekend, and of course I explained to him he was too sick to play. Gene replied, 'Put that liar on the phone.'

"As you can see, I have a lot of leverage in our marriage."

According to Debbie, some of Don's passions are:

• Playing or practicing golf every day, rain or shine.

• Recording the televised golf tournaments and analyzing every swing.

• Watching golf videos or reading golf books at least two hours every night.

• Hanging out at Fiddler's Green (golf shop) to test and/or buy their latest equipment.

• Calling golf pros anywhere in the U.S. for 'The Secret.'
• Planning every day around golf; i.e., appointments, trips, work, etc.

Adds Debbie: "I would say being married to The Prez has made me a very independent person. Also his joy because his love for golf is contagious. He is a very happy person. I would only trade him in, say, one or two days a week."

Meanwhile back at the marriage counselor.....the counselor listened to Debbie, then to Rosy, and concluded that he would have to give up golf if the marriage was to be salvaged. Rosy swallowed hard, and agreed. On the way to the parking lot, however, Rosy turned to Debbie and said, "Honey, we need to find another marriage counselor." Amazingly, Debbie agreed. They arranged to meet with another marriage counselor, who listened to both sides of the controversy, then turned to Debbie and said, "Debbie, there is only one way to save this marriage. You have to become a golfer. This guy is never going to give up golf."

Believe it or not, that's just what she did. Debbie became a golfer, and the Roses have lived happily ever after. It reminds me of Dear Abby's advice to a reader who found herself in a similar predicament. She said, "Never give a golfer an ultimatum unless you're prepared to lose."

So, you think you play a lot of golf? Here's a letter I received from The Prez in 1988, when he was still employed full-time: "Dear Founder, Here's a typical couple of weeks for The Prez:

Saturday, August 26th: Played in the Willamette Valley Chapman. Drove to Columbia Edgewater Country Club and hit balls for three hours. Went home and watched golf tapes until 1 a.m.

Sunday, August 27th: Played second round of Willamette Valley Chapman. Hit two large buckets of balls.

Monday, August 28th: Drove five hours to Medford, OR. and played practice round for Southern Oregon Amateur. Hit balls for two and a half hours, then putted in the moonlight until 9:30 p.m.

Tuesday, August 29th: Played another practice round. Hit balls for two and a half hours, then putted in the moonlight until 9:30 p.m.

Wednesday, August 30th: Played qualifying round for match play. Hit balls 'til dark.

Thursday, August 31st: Won first match. Putted and chipped 'til dark.

Friday, September 1st: Won second match. Called teaching pro Jerry Mowlds for some pointers.

Saturday, September 2nd: Lost match. Very upset. Hit balls with new clubs. Tried 14 putters. Called another teaching pro to arrange golf lesson.

Sunday, September 3rd: Drove three hours to Emerald Valley Golf Course and played 18 holes. Practiced 'til dark.

Monday, September 4th: Played 36 holes.

Tuesday, September 5th: Called Jerry Mowlds on the spur of the moment, arranged for a lesson, and drove two hours to Portland, Oregon for the lesson. Hit the ball perfectly. Thought I had found 'The Secret.'

Wednesday, September 6th: Played golf 'til dark. Very pleased with new swing thoughts.

Thursday, September 7th: Very excited. Men's Day at Eugene C.C. Teed it up with the boys after hitting every practice ball perfectly. Shot an easy 85. Could have been 90 with a missed putt here or there. Oh, death, where is thy hook?"

Don Rose, says Golf Nut member Scott Masingill, is "one of the coolest, funniest men that I have ever met. And the funniest thing I have ever seen probably can't be put into print."

No, it can't. I was there, and it was hilarious. And if I allowed it to be printed, Rosy might never play another round of golf at his beloved Eugene Country Club. Let's just say that we all had a good laugh at Rosy's expense when he putted his first putt off the front of the green. Then he got even with us after he holed his next putt from off the green. Enough said.

"I have every book and video ever published on the golf swing," The Prez says. "And I read them over or look at a video probably once a day. When I watch golf on the tube, I slow motion every swing because I like to check out the mechanical positions.

"I always swing just like the last thing I read or looked at and I always ask everyone I play with how my swing looks. I probably know more about the golf swing than most pros. And I really believe most instructors teach just like the swing feels to them. Hogan and Leadbetter screwed up my swing more than anyone. I love what Jim Flick, Bob Toski, Manuel De La Torre and Sam Snead say about the swing. In other words, I try to just swing the club. Period. You could say the club swings me. I really believe I have 'The Secret.' It's just that the human body can't always do what you want it to. I know my swing is better now than at any time since I started playing this great game.

"To make a long story short, which is hard for me to do, my goal is to swing the club ala Ernest Jones, the director of the Swing the Clubhead Theory of Instruction. And that, to me, is 'The Secret.'"

"Don Rose is probably the biggest fruitcake under the Christmas tree," says Joe Malay, the first Golf Nut of the Year. "He's vocal. He's old. He's tall and he looks like Big Bird with a 2 handicap. He scares little people because of his age."

"I think I need a longer shaft."

5th Hole

"JOE"

"Joe." That's what everybody calls him. Just "Joe."

If you get his answering machine, he will identify himself as "George Dubya Bush." And it will confuse you. If he calls you back, he will identify himself as "Joe Malay, Weiser, Idaho."

He will apologize and tell you, "I'm in and out more than wind through my grandmother."

There is only one Joe Malay. In Weiser they recently held the 50th annual fiddle festival. "There are 5,208 people in Weiser," Joe says. "5,000 of them know me and I know the other 208."

If you say to a golfer in Idaho, "Have you seen Joe lately?" they know exactly who you're talking about. It was serendipity that Joe Malay and I should meet, completely by accident, only a few short weeks after the Golf Nuts Society was created. There we were, on the first tee of Eugene Country Club, two of my friends and I, preparing to tee off in a practice round for the 1986 Pacific Coast Amateur. About twenty yards to our left was the practice putting green, and standing on the green was a guy in a clown outfit. Well, it certainly looked like a clown outfit. I made the fatal mistake of making eye contact with him, and he asked, "Hey, how ya doin'? Can I join you guys?"

"Uh...sure. Where'd you get the outfit?"

"Downtown Weiser! har!, har!, har!"

As we were walking down the first fairway (actually, we hadn't even gotten off the front of the tee), he asked, "Where'd you get that bag tag?"

A match had been made in heaven.

That was my introduction to the legendary Joe Malay, reigning Idaho Amateur Champion, and one of the longest drivers in the game. You'd be long too, if you swung a 48-inch driver with a valve stem inserted into the top of the grip (58 psi, before you ask.) Of course, you've got to be strong enough to swing a 48-inch driver, and Joe is plenty strong.

Joe Malay doesn't have a job. "Well, it's a problem," he says. "It would have a negative effect on my golf. You see, I love golf too much to work, and golf and work are incompatible. I love to play in golf tournaments, so that's what I do. I plan to get a job when I'm too old to play."

"His source of income?" you say. "To be determined at a later date," says Joe. "I'm independently happy."

He turned 54 on "July 23rd and 24th, 2002," he says. "My mother thought I was born on the 23rd," he says. "Then I found out it was the 24th at 12:01 a.m. I'm the oldest teenager in Weiser, spelled just liked the beer but without the Bud."

Joe Malay has always marched to the beat of a different drummer. He lives in Weiser, a small town in western Idaho, and everybody knows Joe. Well, except his wife, Mary. Joe isn't home a lot during the golf season, so when someone calls and asks, "Where's Joe?" Mary replies, "I don't know, let me check the IGA (Idaho Golf Association) schedule." Need we say more?

Every golf nut needs an understanding wife, but Mary breaks all the records. Joe played in 53 tournaments in 1986, and the tournament season is only nine months long. That adds up to almost six tournaments a month. In fact, he'll often play in two tournaments on the same weekend, getting a morning tee time in one, and an afternoon tee time in the other. Joe gets in plenty of practice rounds too. He averages over 300 rounds of golf a year, and that's done in only nine months, since it gets pretty cold in Idaho in the winter. If you run the numbers you'll see that Joe averages 38 18-hole rounds of golf a month. The final tournament of the year for Joe is the Pneumonia Open.

Speaking of cold weather, one bitter cold day in the dead of winter Joe decided he needed a round of golf to keep from going nuts. The temperature was 18 degrees, the wind was blowing at 20 mph, the fairways, greens, and water hazards were frozen solid, and the flagsticks were frozen in the cups. Joe shot an unbelievable 62 at Gem County Muni in Emmett, Idaho, and that was with a ball out-of-bounds on one hole!

Yes, Joe can play. He won the 1986 Idaho Amateur and dozens of other tournaments during his storied career. But Joe is best known for his wardrobe and his antics. He dresses like a rodeo clown, and makes all of his own outfits. If Joe shows up wearing two socks of the same color, he obviously dressed in the dark.

And all of his pants are knee-length. So it's not hard to spot Joe from several fairways over, and if you ask him where he got the outfit, he answers, "Downtown Weiser." Joe once received a pair of brand new $75 slacks that his benefactor had received as a birthday gift from his wife. "Joe, only you would have the courage to wear these pants," he said.

One of Joe's most famous antics was the time he had to charter a crop duster to fly him to a tournament. Joe was on his way to the Treasure Valley Open in Caldwell, Idaho, from his home in Weiser, when he got a flat tire. The spare, it turned out, was flat, too. Undaunted, Joe threw his clubs over his shoulder, walked to the nearest farmhouse, got a ride to the airport, and hired the local crop duster to fly him to the tournament for $85.

As they flew over the course, Joe saw that his group was on the tee, and told the pilot to fly low over the small lake on the course, saying that he was going to jump in the lake with his clubs over his shoulder. Fortunately, the pilot talked him out of it, took him to the Boise airport where Joe grabbed a cab, gave the driver $10 for a $3 fare and said, "Run all the lights!" Joe arrived at the first tee just in time to see his group walking toward the first green. They had already hit their second shots, and Joe had to be disqualified. "No problem," said Joe, "I just left my clubs with one of the officials, and caddied for a friend for the next four days."

Speaking of caddying, Joe was named the "Best-Dressed Caddie" in the 1980 U.S. Open by one of the USGA officials. He was caddying for friend and fellow golf nut Scott Masingill, who had qualified for the event. Joe caught the attention of everyone— officials and spectators alike.

My favorite story about Joe, though, is the time he qualified for the Sunnehanna Amateur in Johnstown, PA, but didn't have the money for the airfare. So he hitchhiked from Weiser to Johnstown. "It only took ten days," says Joe, "But they were getting a little worried since I was the last one to arrive and nobody knew where I was, including my wife."

As you read earlier, Joe is also well known for his drivers. They range in length from 48 to 60 inches, but his most infamous driver was the 48-inch 9.5 degree Taylor Made Tour Burner with a reverse-wrapped carbon graphite shaft. It's the one with the valve stem inserted into the top of the grip. Joe Malay, you see, hits it pretty hard. And he kept caving in the steel head of his driver. So he decided that the club just needed a little rein-forcement.

How did he do this? He made sure that there was plenty of epoxy down where the club head joins the shaft, inserted the valve stem in the grip, took the club down to the local service station, and pumped it up to about 58 psi.

Suddenly he could hit it just as hard as he wanted. He checked with the USGA to make sure it was legal. It is—as long as you don't change the air pressure while you play. Joe Malay claims to be the only golfer in the world who has ever carried an air pressure gauge in his golf bag.

Joe once made a hole-in-one in a tournament, but on the wrong hole. They were giving away a brand new car for a hole-in-one on No. 3, and Joe made a hole-in-one on the 16th. Joe talked the car dealer into letting him drive the car for a week if he promised to leave the name of the dealer painted on the windows of the car.

In spite of Joe's heavy schedule and obvious priorities, he still finds time to involve himself in numerous charitable and civic activities. Joe is a living legend in Idaho, and a credit to the game of golf. In fact, in 1986 he received the Jefferson Award, a national recognition award by the Reagan Administration, for his civic and charitable work around Idaho.

"Joe's secret, for my money, is his heart," says Don Rose, The Prez. "It's big and wide and he is always up. He backs up his great sense of humor with sincerity and love for everyone. His quick mind, to come up with his remarks and off-the-cuff jokes, always cracks everyone up and then he really gets going. He is the worst chipper and putter I have ever seen. But, for just plain fun, he is awesome."

Ah, yes, the sense of humor. "Ron Garland is Mr. Khaki and I'm Mr. Tacky," Joe says. "I've had trick-or-treaters come to my house dressed as me. I'm hollered at and recognized in Weiser. I scare a lot of people at first."

Joe Malay was also the first official "Golf Nut of the Year."

"It was an honor," he says. "I am a golfer and I am a nut. My nut points accrue naturally. I don't go out and do things to accumulate nut points. But there aren't many people in the United States or the world who have their name on that trophy. Michael Jordan's name is under mine on that trophy. I'm proud to be a golf nut."

And we're proud that he was our first-ever Golf Nut of the Year.

"But Michael, what about your MVP trophy?"

6th Hole
MICHAEL JORDAN, NUT #0023

Michael Jordan has been a great friend of the Golf Nuts Society over the years. It all started in late 1986, only a few short months after the Society had been founded. And it was blind luck.

Peter Moore (#0002), as you recall, was the creative director of Nike, and one of his jobs was to create an "image" and a branding campaign for the athletes that Nike was attempting to sign to endorsement contracts.

Once this image—and the branding and marketing program surrounding it—had been created, the athletes would make their way to Nike headquarters in Beaverton, OR and check out what Nike had in store for them if they should sign.

In 1984 there was a pretty good basketball player from the University of North Carolina who had decided to test his skills in the NBA. After Michael Jordan signed with Chicago, it was a bidding war for his endorsement, and Nike was making a full-court press for his services. On several occasions during the summer of 1986, Michael came to Oregon to meet with Nike, and Peter Moore was one of the people at Nike who worked closely with Michael when he visited Nike headquarters. However, there was this one small problem: Michael was good until about noon, and then he wanted to be on the golf course. Peter was aware of Michael's absolute requirement, and so he arranged for me to host Michael on several occasions that summer. The first time I teed it up with Jordan, Peter was in the foursome. When we arrived at the 18th tee, Peter said, "Michael, Ron just started a club that's perfect for you."

"Yeah? What's it called?"

"The Golf Nuts Society."

"The what?"

"The Golf Nuts Society. You know, Golf Nuts, like you."

Then I decided to put in my two cents' worth and said, "Yep, and I'll be happy to give you a free membership."

He looked at me like I was nuts, and responded, "No, man, you don't understand. You gotta pay me."

I replied, "No, man, you don't understand. I can't afford you."

He laughed, and said, "Okay, sign me up. What do I get?"

"A bag tag, a membership card, and our entrance exam. And you can have some of our products if you want them."

He ended up taking four "Registered Golf Nut" license plate frames, and later told me that he had put them on the front and rear plates of two of his cars.

That's how it all got started with the greatest basketball player—and perhaps the biggest golf nut—of all time. He had the disease real bad. He just couldn't get enough golf. When he came to town I would ask him what he'd done since I last saw him that might be worth Nut points, and he would rattle off some of the most amazing things. Here are just a few of the incredible golfing feats of Nut #0023:

During his days as a basketball legend, Michael Jordan played no basketball during the off-season. He was too busy playing golf. Even when he traveled to a variety of places across the globe, his clubs always accompanied him. Michael played more than 150 rounds of golf during his four-month off-season in 1989. That's 37.5 rounds a month, dude.

And he pulled it off despite his heavy off-season promotional and business commitments. He also played in five PGA Tour-related and 12 charity events during the summer of 1989, which was probably indicative of the way every summer was for Michael. I think we can net it out by saying that he plays golf or hits balls every day during the off-season.

When Michael Jordan arrives home he's not far from golf either. He has an indoor putting green, a nine-hole outdoor putting green, and an indoor golf center, complete with driving net, high-speed video camera, and computerized golf swing analyzer. And all of these are in his house.

He's been seen on more than one occasion practicing his swing in front of the picture window in the front yard of his Chicago home in the dead of winter in below-freezing temperatures.

Michael's appetite for playing golf is legendary. In 1988 he played in the Fred Meyer Challenge Pro-Am in Portland, then drove across town to another golf course and played until dark, then boarded a Learjet the next morning and flew to Vail, CO where he teed off that afternoon in the Jerry Ford Invitational Pro-Am.

On another occasion in 1988 he hosted his Michael Jordan Charity Golf Classic in North Carolina, then took a "red-eye" to Portland where he played the following morning in the United Cerebral Palsy charity event. He then skipped the post-round dinner and played until dark, caught a late-night flight to Seattle where he enjoyed a friendly foursome match with friends the following morning.

Three rounds in three cities in three days, coast-to-coast. That's nuts.

One of my favorite memories of golf with Michael was the time that I picked him up at Nike around 1:00 p.m. for an afternoon of golf. We teed off at two, and finished at 10 in total darkness, 45 holes later. One of the most intriguing things about playing golf with someone like Michael is that you get a view of a mega-celebrity's life from inside the fishbowl. It was interesting to watch the day develop, since Peter Moore and I always made a point of not announcing to anyone that Michael Jordan was going to be playing. However, it didn't make much difference, because it was only a matter of time until everyone knew that "He" was on the course.

When we teed off that afternoon only a handful of people in the pro shop and the surrounding area were aware that Michael was at the course. When we made the turn the first time, there were 15-20 people standing behind the ninth green, and another dozen or so watching as we teed off on the 10th.

As we made the turn the second time, there were people everywhere. The word was out.

The tenth tee is right next to the clubhouse restaurant, which is right beside the club swimming pool. It was a warm summer day, and as we approached the clubhouse after finishing the front nine for the second time I asked Michael if he wanted a sandwich. He said, yes, but then took a look at the crowd as we pulled up to the 10th tee and said, "Forget it, let's go."

He had obviously been in this type of situation before. There were people standing on the veranda and near the tee. There were people with their noses pressed up against the inside of the restaurant window. And there were dozens of people hanging over the swimming pool wall.

I said, "I'm sorry Michael, this happens to me every time I make the turn out here."

"Yeah, right. Hit it," he laughed.

We played another 18 and then Peter Moore and Gregg Guernsey joined us for the final 18. The last few holes were really dark. On the final hole we literally had to play by feel. It didn't even do any good to have someone stand behind the guy hitting. It was pitch black. It was so dark that we set off a motion detector light in one of the backyards along the fairway.

We all teed off, and the barbs were flying. We were all convinced that we had hit good drives, and when we got up to where they had landed, unbelievably, they were all in the fairway. We hit our second shots, and again everyone had their mouths going about how well we had hit our approaches. So the bet was on ($1 for closest to the hole.) As we approached the green we could see that one of the balls was only a foot from the hole, and Michael started laughing and pointing, convinced that it was his.

He jumped out of the cart and ran to the green and picked up the ball. It was mine. He looked at it, uttered an expletive, and fired it back down the fairway. "That'll be one dollar," I announced calmly.

After the round(s), Michael showered, we played some pool in the clubhouse, and then Peter took him to the airport for an 11:15 p.m. flight to Chicago. He flew all night, arriving at 5:30 a.m., and drove directly to Olympia Fields Golf Club, where he played another 54 holes of golf. That was a grand total of 99 holes in less than 24 hours in two cities half a continent apart. No wonder he was 1989 Golf Nut of the Year.

Now we all know about Michael's legendary competitiveness. One of the great stories about him was the time he gave a baggage handler a big tip to make sure that his bags came off the conveyor first so he would win a bet with his teammates. I've had the good fortune of witnessing his competitive streak firsthand on a number of occasions.

One day when Michael was in town for a game against the Portland Trailblazers, Peter Moore and I teed it up with him on the day before the game. It was a beautiful, sunny day in Portland (a rarity), and we had a great time. The third hole at the club is a dogleg-left par 4 with a creek that runs along the left side and crossing the fairway just beyond the landing area. We had all hit our second shots, and as we approached the bridge I decided to have a little fun. The creek was about 15-18 feet wide and only about a foot or two deep, so I issued a challenge.

"Michael, I'll bet you can't jump that creek."

"How much?" he replied.

"Five bucks."

"You're on!"

Now, as this little scene is developing, Peter is standing watching in silent amazement. But as Michael started going into his stance, Peter jumped in and hollered, "Wait a minute. I don't want to read about this in the newspapers tomorrow. That's all I need; MJ breaking his ankle while playing golf with me."

Logic prevailed, and the bet was canceled. Well—postponed until the back nine, actually. The rest of the day was filled with one "do/don't" after another—Michael's favorite kind of bet. Here's the way it works: Michael says, "Do/don't for $5 to hit the fairway." He is betting that you can't hit the fairway, and he can. The one who hits the fairway wins the $5. If both players hit the fairway, there's no blood. It was do/don't on long drives; do/don't for being in the fairway; do/don't on closest to the pin; do/don't on putts, etc., etc., etc.

It was a blast, and it was a firsthand look at a man who absolutely thrived on pressure. A do/don't is exactly like a last-second shot to win the game, and he loved the moment. I can't tell you how many times I watched him make an improbable shot or a clutch putt to win the do/don't. It was a lesson in positive thinking from one of the greatest athletes in history.

As we approached the 17th green I just had to see that competitive mind-set one more time, so I said, "Michael, I'll bet you that I can beat you to the green."

"You're on!" he said once again. But this time there was no creek, and Peter let the competition commence. We were about a hundred yards from the front of the green, and I said, "All right, we'll start from here." And we both got into our sprinter's stances.

"I'll count to three and we'll go on three," I announced. He agreed.

I started my count; "One, two. . .". and I took off, giving myself about a five-yard head start.

"Hey!" he yelled, and took off after me. He went past me like a bullet train, and I was another $5 lighter. But it was worth every penny. He is fast!

One of Michael's most celebrated NBA incidents also involved golf. In 1988, Michael was named the NBA's Most Valuable Player. On the day of the MVP award presentation, then-commissioner Larry O'Brien flew to Chicago to make the presentation, along with a whole host of other NBA management officials and media types, as well as top management and coaches for the Chicago Bulls. Unfortunately, Michael wasn't there. He was at Pinehurst Golf Resort in North Carolina playing 36 holes of golf. He had been at Pinehurst since the day after the NBA season ended, and hadn't bothered to tell anyone from the NBA or the Chicago Bulls that he wouldn't be attending the ceremony.

Michael began each day at Pinehurst with a 7:30 a.m. lesson, followed by 18 holes of golf, followed by a one-hour practice session on the range. After lunch, another hour of practice, followed by a second 18 holes, followed by yet another hour of practice. This continued for two consecutive weeks—the final total being 504 holes of golf and who knows how many practice balls. Now that's nuts.

The 1989 season wasn't much different from 1988, except this time Jordan didn't "no-show" for his MVP award. The Bulls went out early in the play-offs, and the day after Michael Jordan's 1989 NBA season ended with a loss in those play-offs, he left Chicago at 5 p.m. and drove all night to Pinehurst (800 miles). The reason? Golf.

He joined friends the next morning for a 10 o'clock tee time and 36 holes of golf, without a wink of sleep the night before. He then drove to Rexford Plantation, South Carolina and played 54 holes a day for four consecutive days. That's 252 holes of golf in five days in two different cities. Go nuts, baby—#0023 can really go.

In the late summer of 1989, Michael invited me to the inaugural "Michael Jordan UNCF Celebrity Classic;" a charity golf tournament at the beautiful La Costa resort in Carlsbad, California. The event was a one-day scramble format, and everyone teed off in the morning in a shotgun start. After the round, we had the afternoon free, followed by an evening black-tie dinner.

As I was hitting a few practice putts on the putting green, Michael came over and asked, "You want to play some more? A few of my friends and I are teeing off right now." As we approached the first tee I saw a couple of familiar faces (famous faces would be a better description!). They belonged to James Worthy of the Lakers and the legendary Julius "Dr. J" Erving, accompanied by four of Michael's high school buddies. Talk about fun.

We played an eightsome—four two-man scramble teams—and for the next nine holes I laughed as much as I've ever laughed on a golf course. The needling was relentless, and the competition was fierce. I don't remember who won, but I do remember that we were all late for the black-tie dinner. But we were with the host, so what were they going to do, start without him? We missed the entire cocktail hour, and were 30 minutes late for the dinner. But we were "golf nuts." That sort of behavior is expected. Isn't it?

It seems that Michael is always getting into trouble for playing too much golf. In 1990 he withdrew from the NBA Slam-Dunk Contest "due to injury," and then played 36 holes of golf the same day. That one made the headlines around the world and got Michael in a little hot water with the NBA, too.

At times Michael's antics make you wonder if he might even like golf more than basketball. One year, two days before the NBA All-Star game in Orlando, Michael was notified by the NBA of a one-game suspension for an altercation in a game against the Utah Jazz. Rather than sit with his team on the bench at the last game before the break, he immediately flew to Orlando and played 36 holes of golf while his Bulls teammates were playing the Phoenix Suns. He also skipped the NBA All-Star Game's "Media Day" that year to play another 36 holes the day before the all-star game.

Ever the competitor, Jordan challenged Mickey Mouse to a putting contest while out on the course. Michael seems to have a thing about all-star breaks. It's one of the few times when NBA players have a break of any length—unless you're the greatest basketball players in the world—and then everybody wants a piece of you. Michael apparently takes a different view of the situation. He sees it as one of those rare occasions when he can play golf all day, and he does it.

When the 1993 All-Star Game was held in chilly Salt Lake City, he skipped "Media Day" and flew to Las Vegas with two other All-Stars to play golf at the famous Shadow Creek Golf Club. When asked why he flew to Las Vegas, he said that the NBA should hold the All-Star Game only in warm-weather cities. Now that's an answer that the Golf Nuts Society enthusiastically endorses.

Another special moment with Michael involved basketball and golf. I had moved to Scottsdale, AZ, in 1990, and in 1993 the Bulls were in the NBA Finals against the Phoenix Suns. The first game in Phoenix was scheduled for a Tuesday, as I recall, and I left a message for Michael that I was now living in the Phoenix area. I mentioned that if he wanted to play golf on the day before the first game, we could play as many holes as he wanted, and we wouldn't be bothered. He returned the call, and the next day we played 36 holes. But it wasn't quite that simple.

Again, there I was, in the fishbowl, but this time it was even more amazing. It started with the phone call to his room that evening to confirm our game. The measures that he has to go through to do just about anything would be too much for most everyone else. He had left a message for me at my home, which I returned when I got home from a business trip. In the message, he had given me his room number along with the hotel's main switchboard number. When I called the switchboard and asked for his room, the operator asked me to tell them whose room I was calling. "Michael Jordan," I replied.

"Thank you, and may I have your name please, sir? I gave her my name, and she said, "One moment please." She was obviously clearing me with Michael. After a few moments he came on the line, we chatted briefly, and arranged the game.

"I have only one question," I said.

"What's that?"

"Are we going 18 or 36?"

"Thirty-six, of course. But there is one small problem."

"What's that?" I asked.

"Well, I have a practice from 12 to 2. How early can we play?"

"The first tee time at our club is 8 a.m."

"Eight o'clock? What kind of club do you belong to?"

"I know, it's a stupid rule. But there won't be anyone on the course that early, and we'll zoom around the course and get you back in plenty of time."

"Okay, pick me up at 7 a.m. When you get here in the morning, go into the lobby and get on a house phone and call my room."

"Okay, see you in the morning."

That was only the beginning. I arrived at the hotel at 7 a.m., picked up the house phone in the lobby, and asked for Michael's room. Same drill, different day. After a few moments, he answered the phone.

"Where are you?"

"In the lobby."

"See if you can get somebody on the phone who works at the hotel. I need to find out where the closest exit is, and have you meet me there."

About that time, a bellman walked by, and I grabbed him, handed him the phone, and said, "Here, this is Michael Jordan. He needs your help."

I thought I was going to have to catch his jaw before it hit the floor. He gulped hard, and said, "Okay."

Michael told him where his room was, and the bellman explained where the nearest exit was, and how to get there from his room. He handed me the phone again, and Michael said, "Okay, wait for me at the side exit, and have the trunk open and the car running."

"What?"

"I'll leave the room in a couple of minutes, as soon as I'm sure you're there."

The bellman then showed me where to park, and I drove around to the side of the hotel. I parked near the side exit, opened the trunk of the car, and leaned against the back of the car, waiting for Michael to appear. It was still dark. A few moments later, Michael came down the outside stairs—almost running—with his clubs over his shoulder.

"Quick, get in!" he yelled.

I bolted for the driver's side of the car and jumped behind the wheel, and Michael threw his clubs in the trunk, slammed it, jumped into the car, and said, "Go!"

Almost as if on cue, people started appearing from out of nowhere. Most of them were young, but not all of them. Some men, some women, and they were chasing us. "Oh my God," I said, amazed at the sight unfolding before my eyes.

"Go! Go! Go!" he said. "We've got to lose them!"

There were probably 15-20 people running after the car. And as we began to leave the resort grounds, two cars started to follow us. I punched it, made a couple of unrehearsed elusive maneuvers, and "lost" them.

"Nice to see you," I said.

"Yeah, nice to see you too. How far to the golf course?"

"About twenty minutes."

"You sure you're gonna get me back to practice on time?"

"No problem."

Such is the glamorous life of a superstar. The guy has no private life. I'm sure it's one of the reasons that he loves golf as much as he does. It's probably the closest he ever comes to being alone when he's outdoors.

We arrived at the golf course, unannounced, grabbed a cart, and teed off. Virtually no one knew that we were there except the assistant pro, who had just opened the shop a few minutes earlier. We had a very pleasant morning, tooling around the course while we kept an eye on the clock (he still had a practice session at noon.) Only one person asked him for an autograph—one of the course maintenance crew—and there were a half-dozen people milling around as we made the turn (it happens everywhere I go!).

I got Michael back to his hotel by 11:00—in plenty of time to make practice. It was only the NBA Finals the next day, what was the big deal? Of course, I had to drop him off at the side entrance. But before he bolted for his room, he said, "Okay, I'll meet you here at two-thirty." He quickly disappeared around the corner and up the stairs.

I went back to my office for a couple of hours, and then returned to the hotel and waited for the team bus to return from practice. This time I wasn't alone. There were at least 200 people waiting too, but they were there only to get a brief glimpse of the Bulls players as they left the bus and went to their rooms. I couldn't help but wonder what it must be like to be locked up in your hotel room so many days of your life.

Anyway, as the players exited the bus and made their way through the crowd, Michael spotted me and nodded, confirming that we were set for Phase II of our excellent adventure. As I waited by the side entrance again, I thought, "How is Michael going to avoid the people this time?"

I got my answer shortly. Michael came down the stairs walking much more slowly and more casually than before. I guess it had a little to do with the huge guy who was coming down the stairs ahead of him. I forget his name, but I won't soon forget his size or the look on his face. He was Michael's personal bodyguard, and needless to say, nobody bothered Michael as he casually dropped his clubs into the trunk and introduced me to his bodyguard. He was actually a very nice man, but he did his job very well, and we left the hotel parking lot without incident.

The afternoon round had again been arranged at my club, but this time I wanted Michael to meet a couple of real Nuts. I had called Duke DeBernardi (#0889) and Ken Kellaney (#2020) earlier in the day and invited them to join us. They were waiting for us on the driving range when we arrived.

"Duke of the Desert," as we refer to him, is one of the nicest guys in the Society, and a very good player. Ken is a five-time state amateur champion (four in Arizona and one in Illinois,) and great guy as well. It was a memorable round. Lots of fun needling, and a very serious best-ball game. Since Ken had lived most of his life in Chicago before moving to Arizona, he and MJ took on the two "desert rats." It was The Head Nut and The Duke versus MJ and KK. And we kicked their butts. It wasn't even close.

To this day, I believe Duke and I were singularly responsible for the Bulls victory in the NBA Finals as Michael bounced back from his resounding defeat at the hands of the "desert rats." Well, it is possible, isn't it?

As the day came to an end, and as we putted out on the 18th green, we were treated to a spectacular sunset. After he putted, Michael walked to the back of the green, stared off in the direction of the sunset, and said to no one in particular, "What a perfect day." You could tell, from the way he said it, that he had really enjoyed his time away from the crowds. What a great feeling to know that I had, in some small way, helped him find the eye of the hurricane for a brief moment in time.

When Michael retired from basketball (the first time) he joined a minor league baseball team. The team played in the Phoenix Fall League, and virtually every afternoon after practice, Michael would play golf with his good friend Roy Green, the former NFL All-Pro wide receiver for the Cardinals. One day I received a phone call from Roy, asking if I would like to tee it up later that week with him and Michael.

Former baseball star Garry Templeton rounded out the foursome, and we played all day long, finishing at dusk again. What makes the day memorable is that it was the day after Michael had been in Chicago to have his jersey retired by the Bulls. Michael got up at 4 a.m. that morning, drove to the airport in Chicago, boarded a private jet, landed in Phoenix and drove 30 miles to the golf course. We were still able to tee off by 9 a.m. Michael does love his golf.

It was another day filled with fun banter and lots of "do/don't" bets. Nothing serious; just $5 here and there, mostly when Michael thought he had the edge. He's the ultimate competitor.

One particular moment stands out in my memory from that day. On the 14th tee I spotted a feather and picked it up and put it in my cap. "What are you doing?" Michael asked.

"Whenever you find a feather on the golf course, it means that you're going to make a birdie,'" I replied. "You put it in your cap, and good luck will follow." He just laughed, but Roy Green, who had been having a particularly difficult day, bought into the theory without hesitation. Roy spotted a feather and quickly put it in his cap. We were pumped. Michael laughed at Roy, made some sort of condescending remark, and teed off. To make a long story short, I made a birdie on the hole, and Roy made his first par of the day, which felt every bit like a birdie to him. Michael didn't say a word. But as we teed off on the next hole, he had a feather in his cap.

One final story about Michael Jordan will tell you about the character of the man. It occurred when Michael was in Utah during the NBA Finals one year. I heard the story from the head pro at Wasatch Mountain Municipal Golf Course a couple of years later, when I noticed a photo hanging on the wall of the pro shop, of Michael playing the course.

I asked the pro who Michael played with that day, and he said, "Michael called the golf course one morning and asked if we could get him out on the course. I told him that we would set him up in a game with a couple of our golf professionals, and Michael said, 'No, just send me out with any group when I get there.'" That's Michael Jordan, Nut #0023.

7th Hole

THESE CELEBRITIES ARE NUTS TOO!

The Golf Nuts Society has been blessed with the involvement of many celebrities. Hey, golf drives everybody nuts, even celebrities. Here are a few stories about my experiences with a few of our totally committed celebrity Nuts.

Bob Hope
Nut #0025

Bob Hope may be "The King of Comedy," but around here he's known as Nut #0025. He's also a Board Member of our society, having accepted a position on the Board in 1989. Here's his letter of acceptance, dated March 28, 1989:

Dear Head Nut,

It's been a big year for me and now I've been elevated to the Board of Directors of the Golf Nuts Society. I've been prepping for this honor for the last 15 years and I'm not surprised by the nomination.

To give you an idea, I now have six putters in my bag made by the boomerang people, and a few thin copper shafts on my woods that I can bend easily either way.

It would be nice if you would identify me as one of "the lunatic fringe of golf." Actually, I've been in the rough for so long it's like my second home.

You're looking for "The Secret?" I'm still looking for my last caddie—after my second tee shot he vanished into the woods and has never been heard from.

Nice hearing from you.

Regards,

Bob Hope

A quick note about our Board of Directors. It was decided at our first Board Meeting that we would forego all future Board Meetings in favor of everyone playing as much golf as possible in an effort to expedite the discovery of "The Secret." We also decided it was a good excuse to play more golf, and that it would set a good example for the members.

Peter Jacobsen
Nut #0022

Peter Jacobsen was the Society's first celebrity member. A native Oregonian, Peter eagerly supports local and regional organizations. He was more than happy to join as a celebrity member and as a member of the Golf Nuts Board of Directors. He is also the person responsible for recruiting two other celebrity members: Jack Lemmon and Huey Lewis.

Always known as a real character on the PGA Tour, Jacobsen gained eternal fame in Great Britain and around the world when he tackled a streaker on the 72nd green of the 1985 British Open at Royal St. George's, England.

Peter is also very well known for his impressions of other PGA Tour stars. It all started in high school and college when he would entertain his teammates on the driving range by imitating the likes of Arnold Palmer, Craig Stadler, Johnny Miller and other Tour players. He continued his shtick when he arrived on Tour, and became a pro-am favorite when he and D.A. Weibring created a comedy routine for pro-am participants as part of the PGA Tour events.

Not content with merely being an "impressionist," Peter Jacobsen became "Jake Trout," rock star, when he formed "Jake Trout & The Flounders." The rock group was comprised of Peter Jacobsen, Mark Lye, and the late Payne Stewart. Peter would take existing pop tunes and rewrite the words with a golf theme. The lyrics were great, and the band was good.

They performed at golf events across America, and even released their own album. Lots of Nut points there, Peter!

Anyone who has ever watched the Fred Meyer Challenge—also known as "Peter's Party"—knows that Peter is plenty "nuts" himself. "The Party" is one of the most popular unofficial events in professional golf. Over the years, the golf and celebrity superstars who participate in the tournament have become famous for "giving it up" for charity. Players have been known to literally give the shirt off their backs to bidders at the raucous auction. As a result, The Fred Meyer Challenge has raised millions of dollars for a variety of charities in Oregon. In the same spirit, Peter has donated some great prizes for the Golf Nuts tournaments, the "big prize" being one of his tour bags personally autographed.

But my favorite story about Peter was when I just happened to mention to him that I had seen him on television in a recent tournament. I told him that I noticed a subtle change in his golf swing, and described what I'd seen. He launched into an animated discussion of what he had done to make the swing change, and we two "golf nuts" went on for perhaps another ten minutes discussing swing theory. Hey, even if you have one of the greatest swings in the world, you can always improve.

Lawrence Taylor
Nut #2270

Lawrence Taylor, the former New York Giant All-Pro linebacker, has had his problems, but boy does he love golf. He keeps his golf clubs and shoes inside the front door of his home so that he never forgets them as he heads out the door. One day he headed from his New Jersey home to Florida for a quick eighteen, and was home for dinner. Now that's nuts.

And on more than one occasion, "LT" has been late for football practice because of a round of golf. Once, he was even late for a game.

"The group in front of me was playing really slow." he said.

"Well, why didn't you quit?" I asked.

"I couldn't do that. I was playing great."

I had the opportunity to play golf with Lawrence Taylor a few years ago, and it was an enlightening experience, to say the least. It was a very tough golf course, especially off the tee, and LT wasn't exactly ropin' his tee ball. But on every single shot Lawrence would do the same thing. It went something like this:

"Okay LT, you can do it. Come on baby, you can do it. Don't worry about that last one, baby. This one's in the fairway, baby. Come on, LT, it's okay. You can do it. Put a good swing on it. Come on, LT. Come on. Okay, here we go."

Wham! He would hit another one in the woods. He would go into the woods, find his ball, and it would start all over again.

"Okay LT, you can do it. Come on baby, you can do it. Don't worry about that last one, LT. Knock it in the hole, LT. Knock it in the hole. You can do it. Put a good swing on it. Come on, LT. Come on. Okay, here we go."

It went on like that all day long, on every shot. All the way to a smooth 93. But, you know, he did hit a few good shots that day, and all I kept thinking during the round was, "No wonder he gets so many sacks."

Here's a guy who lines up time after time at the line of scrimmage, and if he has a good game he might sack the quarterback once or twice. I can just imagine: "Okay LT, you can do it. Come on baby, get him this time. Forget the last down, LT. Get him this time, LT. Get him, LT. Get him. Now!"

Roy Green
Nut #2276

Roy Green clearly belongs in our small band of rebels. You've already heard the feather story about Roy, but it speaks volumes about him. Roy will try anything if he thinks it will improve his swing. First, let me say Roy Green's swing will never win "Best Swing on Tour," but it doesn't keep him from trying to improve it.

I remember playing Gainey Ranch in Phoenix one time with "Duke of the Desert," and we got backed up on one hole. When the group behind us caught up to us on the tee, it turned out to be Roy and a buddy of his. I just happened to have a swing training gadget with me in the cart, and Roy spotted it. So before we teed off, there we were, two golf nuts talking swing theory and taking turns with the training gadget. Roy was hanging on my every word. Of course, he had no idea I was just as lost as he was. Why do you think I had the swing gadget in my cart?

"Nellie"
Nut #2709

Roy takes lessons from "Nellie," the Golf Nuts Society's Director of Instruction. And Nellie has some great Roy Green stories.

Nellie's a little nuts himself. Here's a guy who once gave 343 golf lessons in a single day – a Golf Nuts Society record. And he's very good, too. I should know, he's my instructor. And if he can soothe a sick mind like mine, he can help anybody.

Nellie's quite the celebrity himself, being most famous for trying to help the likes of Charles Barkley and Roy Green, as well as being the swing coach of a number of touring pros, too. People like Tim Herron, Tommy Armour III, and a bunch of PGA Tour hopefuls.

Shelby Futch
Nut #2026
Another celebrity instructor is Shelby Futch. "I hate this game," he says. "But it's the only thing I enjoy doing."

It's one of the greatest quotes in the history of golf, because it describes brilliantly the dilemma that we golf nuts endure almost constantly.

And the quote comes from one of the biggest golf nuts on the planet. Shelby Futch is the founder of John Jacobs' Practical Golf Schools, the world's largest golf school. Headquartered in Scottsdale, they annually host huge numbers of golfers at their many schools all over the world. *Golf* Magazine ranks Shelby as one of America's Top 100 golf instructors. He was also one of the pioneers—if not the pioneer— of off-course golf retail shops, with his "Shelby's Golf Shops" in the Chicago area many years ago. Then he met the legendary British golf instructor John Jacobs when they were both instructors at a *Golf Digest* school. A short time later they launched "John Jacobs Practical Golf Schools."

Shelby and I were both members of the same golf club when I lived in Arizona, and we spent many hours together on the driving range, searching for "The Secret." Well, I searched for "The Secret," and he helped me with my search. He was fond of driving up to the back of the range when I was out there beating balls, filming my swing, and saying, "I see you've got the Bunsen burner fired up again."

One of my favorite memories of those days was the time—a couple of weeks before the club championship—that I was hitting balls on the driving range after a lesson with another pro who will remain nameless. I was hitting the ball about as poorly as a human can possibly hit it, and was getting very frustrated. The clubhouse's bar looks out onto the driving range, and unknown to me, Shelby was sitting at the bar having a drink. After I had been (mis)hitting balls for about a half-hour, I heard a voice behind me say, "Ron, what are you trying to do?"

"I took a lesson about a week ago and I've been trying to swing more upright, and I'm hitting it like ****!"

"I know, I've been watching from the bar. What happened to your natural swing? It was fine."

After a few minutes, he had me hitting it great, and I won the club championship. Go figure.

Shelby Futch is one of the nicest people in golf, and a very committed golf nut. Shelby's son, T.J. Futch (#2347) is a celebrity in his own right, being the current holder of the GNS Heat Index record. T.J. played 88 holes in a single day on which the temperature climbed to 118 degrees. Wow.

Chuck Hogan
Nut #0611

Chuck has the dubious distinction of being the man responsible for trying to unscramble my brain. He made a valiant effort, but after several attempts over many years, we both concluded that I had no brain.

Chuck is clearly one of the most brilliant minds in golf. A teaching professional who has a special affinity for the mental aspects of golf, he has written several books, was the founder of Sports Enhancement Associates, and was one of the early pioneers in the area of "sports psychology" (you know, the art of getting out of your own way on the golf course) — even though he dislikes the term.

His video instruction classic, "Nice Shot!" was rated five stars by Golf Magazine (their highest rating) upon its release several years ago.

Chuck Hogan has worked with a number of great players over the years, including Ray Floyd, Johnny Miller, Peter Jacobsen and others. He continues to lecture, write, and to teach golfers of all skill levels from his home in Redmond, Oregon (www.chuckhogan.com).

Chuck remains one of my favorite Nuts because of his unique perspective toward golf, and his even better sense of humor. When I went to see him once for a lesson, he had a tiger's tail hanging out of the gas tank door. Go Nuts.

8th Hole

GOLF NUT GREATS

Jack Nicklaus was great, but did he ever play 280 holes of golf in a single day? Arnold Palmer was great, but did he ever make a gold ball marker from some of the gold in his fillings and keep it in a safe deposit box at the local bank? Tiger Woods is great, but did he ever achieve the Golf Nut Slam?

There are greats and then there are golf nut greats. I, for one, prefer the latter. These are real people, but they'll never win the real Grand Slam—or even the U.S. Open for that matter—but they sure know how to score.

They're middle-aged middle-handicappers, for the most part, who love the game so much that they just can't get enough of it. Some of them can play, too. "I have participated in more than 1,500 golf tournaments and won 200 of them," says Joe Malay, the first Golf Nut of the Year. "I have a zero handicap and have won eight state titles. My point is you can be a nut no matter what your handicap is. Your index or ability doesn't matter."

Golf Nuts play in all kinds of weather, and they've changed their golf swings more often than it rains in Seattle. They've come home late for dinner so often that they've been threatened with divorce because of it. If they hear someone talk about a new high-tech "wonder club," they own it before the sun sets.

They're "nuts." Golf nuts. But some of them have risen to heights never before imaginable. They have become icons within their peer group: The Golf Nuts Society. They are the past winners of the Golf Nut of the Year award, and members of the Golf Nut Hall of Fame. They are Golf Nut Greats, and I'd like to introduce you to a few:

Patrick O'Bryan
1987 Golf Nut of the Year
Patrick O'Bryan took a one-month golf vacation to the British Isles one year, and never looked back. At the end of the month, Patrick called his boss and said, "I quit." And he just kept on playing. It turned into an eight-month golfing odyssey spanning 20 countries and 67 golf courses, and ultimately led to a career change. He returned from his eight-month odyssey hooked on golf, and started a travel business specializing in golf vacations in order to support his habit, which costs him more than $10,000 annually. Patrick already has played more than 140 golf courses on four continents since 1981.

In one three-week span he traveled 33,000 miles to play the world's highest-altitude, lowest altitude, southernmost, northernmost, easternmost and westernmost golf courses. While on this voyage, he arranged a putting competition in the aisle of the airplane as it crossed the International Dateline.

Patrick's nomadic wanderings across the fairways of the world have inspired his mother to create a needlepoint depicting him as a golf bum. Patrick is truly "nuts about golf," and will be remembered as one of the all-time greats.

David Mikkelson
1988 Golf Nut of the Year
David Mikkelson of Seattle was a different kind of golf nut. He just couldn't seem to get enough of this crazy game, so every morning he would rise at 5:30 a.m., meet one of his buddies at a local restaurant for

breakfast, then drive the 30 miles to Mt. Si Golf Course in Snoqualmie, WA for a round of golf. But he wouldn't stop after just one round. Quite often it was 54 holes, in his trusty golf cart that he named "Blue Birdie." Blue Birdie was special. She was equipped with optional features that included a heater, stereo tape deck, curtains, a clock, compass, thermometer, and an assortment of flags.

Dave and Blue Birdie logged over 2,200 rounds and more than 9,000 miles together over the years. Dave was prolific. He averaged 449 rounds a year for six consecutive years, and that was in rainy Seattle. In fact, two years in a row he won the USGA's "GHIN Award" for posting the most rounds played by any golfer in America in a given year. One month he played 56 rounds of golf. And in that same year, 1983, he played 501 rounds of golf while (in his spare time) painting his house.

He had set a goal at the beginning of the year to play 500 rounds of golf, but when December arrived it was a particularly cold month and the snow covered all of the courses in the area. Finding himself short of his goal of 500 rounds, he and his wife flew to California, where he closed out the year with 501 rounds played. Speaking of his wife, Helen was named "World's Greatest Golf Widow" by the Mt. Si Golf Course members.

David didn't let a little pain get in the way of his golf either. He played all of his golf despite suffering from arteriosclerosis, and when David was diagnosed with cancer in 1987, he continued to play golf to the very end, despite weekly chemotherapy treatments.

David Mikkelson exemplified the true golf nut. He dearly loved and was committed to the game of golf, and dreamed of one day being named Golf Nut of the Year. In 1988, David realized that dream. Those of us who share his love of the game will not soon forget him. David died of cancer on August 2, 1988.

Michael Jordan
1989 Golf Nut of the Year

David Earl
1990 Golf Nut of the Year

David Earl lived life big. Who else would go to The Masters every year, and then leave on Friday in order to be at his home club in New York for the traditional first tee time of the season. Yes, his regular foursome would tee it up at 6:30 a.m. on April 7th every year and play 18 holes, regardless of the weather.

And who else can boast that they had teed it up with the president of Augusta National Golf Club—or with Bill "Caddyshack" Murray. A talented writer, Earl chose golf as his profession, and became a golf writer. He soon rose to Managing Editor of *Golf* Magazine, and then Managing Editor of the USGA's official publication, *Golf Journal.* He was also the only golf writer with an endorsement contract (Michelob).

David belonged to six golf clubs (Royal North Devon, Garrison, Waterville, Isles of Sicily, Montclair, and Flamingo Gaze), with an application pending at a seventh. Which brings to mind one of his more amazing feats. He awoke one day at 6:00 a.m. in New York and put in a full day at the office, then drove to the airport and boarded a flight to London. Upon arrival, he rented a car and drove to Royal North Devon and played 18 holes of golf, finally getting to sleep 47 hours after his day had begun in New York.

But David knew how to play too. On a vacation to Hilton Head with a foursome of golf buddies, they played 126 holes of golf in four days, which isn't all that impressive until we learn that the wind chill factor brought the temperatures down to the low 20s everyday. On one day, he and his partners had the first tee time at Haig Point Resort on the coldest morning of the trip. The starter asked, "Are you guys from Alaska?"

I had the opportunity to play a round of golf with David in 1991, at a golf course famous for its tough "common Bermuda" rough. After leaving several chips short of the green, he said to me, "What do you call this stuff!?" "Common Bermuda," I replied. To which he responded, "I've been to Bermuda; they don't have this s**t down there!"

David Earl died of a heart attack on October 2, 1994 at the young age of 48, while in Versailles, France covering the World Amateur Team Championship. Surviving him were his bride of less than a year, Evelyn, and her son, Sean. It is our hope that he is teeing it up daily with his regular foursome of Bobby Jones, Walter Hagen, and Francis Ouimet, hickories in hand.

Pat Seelig
1991 Golf Nut of the Year

Pat Seelig started his golf nut training early. While in high school he would often go to the golf course on sunny days instead of class, and then use his mother's stationery to write his own absence excuse, forging her signature. Amazingly, he never missed a day of school when golf matches were scheduled.

Not quite good enough to make his college golf team on scholarship, he was a "walk-on", and made the team, playing in only one match in three years. But that wasn't the goal. He wanted the all-important free golf exemption at the more exclusive clubs in the area, and he got it. This strategy surfaced again as an adult when he arranged for his wife to get a job at EDS in Dallas, because they had an employee golf course that allowed spouses to play as well.

Perhaps nothing speaks to Pat's priorities better than his reaction after nearly being killed in an automobile accident. He awoke in the ambulance and asked, "Where are my clubs?" Pat is a sportswriter, but like so many golf nuts, he always had a dream of being a tour player. However, the closest he ever got was the time he quit his job as a sports editor to become a caddie on the LPGA Tour. Unfortunately, he got fired in his first tournament when he told his player that he could beat her.

Pat is a traditionalist, refusing to ride in a golf cart unless absolutely forced to do so by club policy. One year at the national Golf Writers

Association of America golf tournament, his steadfastness was put to the ultimate test. (He passed with flying colors.)

Refusing to ride in a cart during the tournament, Pat was banned from Wild Dunes Resort for a year, but finished the tournament as the only contestant who walked and carried his bag.

"Golf is my life, my income, my passion," says Pat. One year he proved he meant what he said. He was fortunate enough to get press credentials for The Masters. However, he was also planning to get married at about the same time, so he convinced his bride-to-be to schedule their wedding two weeks before The Masters so they could celebrate their honeymoon in Augusta.

Merle Ball
1992 Golf Nut of the Year

A skeptic would look at some of Merle Ball's accomplishments and say "no way." For starters, Merle claims that in 1991 he played 1,290 rounds of golf AND hit 65,800 practice balls. Now if you take a calculator to those two numbers here's what you get: to play 1,290 rounds of golf in a single year, Merle would have had to play 3.53 rounds of golf everyday during the year. That's 69 holes a day. Every day. But then you add to that his 65,800 practice balls, and that averages out to 180 balls a day. Hmm...I'm not sure about this one. But I met Merle in 1995, and he seemed like a perfectly honest guy to me. And he did have a lot of energy, especially for a 77-year-old. But these numbers would be astounding even for a 27-year-old.

Merle didn't take up golf seriously until he retired, at age 65, but he quickly made up for lost time with his incredible escapades. His loving wife, Mildred, who accompanied him through most of his record-breaking activities, likes to say of Merle, "He worked hard for forty years; why shouldn't he be allowed to play just as hard?"

Merle is what we golfers call a "character." In other words, he enjoys being just a little bit different from everyone else. He plays golf both right-handed and left-handed, and uses a cross-handed grip when playing right-handed. Just to lend credence to his unique ways, in 1988 Merle played golf right-handed in all 50 states. Then in 1989, he switched to the other side, and played golf in all 50 states left-handed, but this time he did it in only 51 days. "We had a weather delay in Seattle on the way to Hawaii, or I would have done it in 50 days." recalled Merle at the time.

Merle was one impressive guy, but my favorite story about him involves his world record. On June 19, 1992, Merle became the first person in history to hit a ball across four states with a single shot. The way he did it proved he's a different kind of golf nut.

Here it is in his words:

"Well, I went over to the Four Corners, where Arizona, Colorado, Utah, and New Mexico meet, and they have this monument that marks the exact spot. So I get me some PVC pipe and make a circle around the mark, put a ball in one end of the PVC pipe and give it a whack with my putter, and went across all four states. So John Daly don't have nuthin' on me."

Merle loved life and loved golf, but not nearly as much as he loved his wonderful and supportive wife, Mildred. He passed away on November 10, 2000 at the age of 82, but he left a legacy that will long be remembered.

E.M. Vandeweghe
1993 Golf Nut of the Year

E.M. Vandeweghe was on the driving range at El Dorado C.C. when I arrived at his home for our introductory meeting. But that's not so odd; he was always on the driving range. Mr. Vandeweghe was 88 years young when I first met him, and had been playing golf since 1919. But what was oddly humorous was my "introduction" to Vandeweghe's passion for golf.

You see, he had told me to meet him at his home but he was at the driving range. Fortunately for me, he lived on Fairway Drive, only five houses from the entrance to the gate of El Dorado Country Club, so I drove to the clubhouse gate and asked the guard where I might find Mr.

Vandcwcghe.

"Right over there," said the guard, as he pointed to a lone figure hitting balls at the end of the driving range.

Vandeweghe brought new meaning to the term "home on the range." He would hit 300 range balls everyday before playing nine or 18 holes. And God forbid that you ever asked him a question about your swing. You would immediately find yourself in a golf lesson that might very well last for the rest of your life!

Vandeweghe began his love affair with golf at Van Cortland Municipal course in New York and practiced daily for the next 50 years. He would regularly "close" the driving range every night. Not satisfied with merely going to the range every day, E.M. built what might be described as the first "home" driving range—before there was such a thing—by putting up a tarp in his backyard. He would get up at six in the morning and hit balls into the tarp. The "thump, thump" of balls would wake up the whole family, not to mention the neighbors.

Winter created a whole new set of problems, so he built an indoor driving range in his garage. Now, 74 years later, at age 88, he lived less than 300 yards from the driving range of his club. Yet he still had a hitting area in his backyard.

One morning, while still living in New York, E.M. was practicing in his backyard driving range when he "got it." His son, Ernie Jr., convinced him not to change his grip or take his hands off the club. He told him he would put the top down on the convertible and drive him to the golf course so he could try his new swing.

They drove the two miles to the course with E.M. holding onto the club in the back seat, never once changing his grip. When he arrived at the course, Ernie Jr. teed up a ball and E.M. took a swipe at it, shanking the ball into the pro shop. It was 7 a.m., and his hands had frozen on the drive to the course.

As of this writing, E.M. Vandeweghe's old football injury has finally taken him to the sidelines, but he still lives for golf and receives our e-mails daily.

Howdy Giles
1994 Golf Nut of the Year

Some ardently committed "golf nuts" cringe at the term, but they are golf nuts nonetheless. Dr. Howdy Giles is one of these. Perhaps the nicest man in all of golf, Howdy is a staunch traditionalist. He loves the game, but he's not sure that he is what we refer to as a "golf nut."

The late Winnie Palmer, Arnold's wife, perhaps had the perfect title for Howdy when she dubbed him the "Commander-In-Chief of Arnie's Army." Every king needs someone to muster the troops, and Howdy is that man. He first met Arnold Palmer in 1970 at the grand opening of one of his Pitch & Putt courses, and had his picture taken with The King. However, the relationship started much earlier. In the mid-'60s Giles's fiancée, Carolyn (now his wife), bought him a set of Arnold Palmer golf clubs. Soon thereafter she began buying all of his clothes from "The Arnold Palmer Collection" at a store called Wanamaker's in Delaware.

Like just about everyone who ever meets The King, Howdy was instantly taken by Palmer's charisma. He became a fan. The relationship has grown to the point that Giles, now Arnie's dentist, has played golf with Arnie more than a hundred times, and flies to The Masters every year in Arnie's Learjet. Giles is also a member of three Palmer-owned or designed golf courses: Bay Hill, Latrobe, and Isleworth.

It got so serious that when Howdy bought a condo at Bay Hill, he bought the one that was located under the unit once occupied by Palmer. Which was the reason he bought it. The other reason he bought the condo was that it was across the driveway from where Arnie lived. And then, to put an exclamation mark on his infatuation with The King, Howdy built a deck on his condo so he could sit on the deck, sip on a beer, and watch Arnie work on his clubs in his garage.

A USGA Rules Official, Giles officiates at most major USGA events. He was there for Palmer's final U.S. Open at Oakmont. He was a house guest at Arnie's home in Latrobe on Tuesday evening of U.S. Open week, and Arnie autographed and gave Howdy the ball he used to sink the birdie putt on the 18th hole on Thursday. It has become a treasured part of a priceless trove of Arnold Palmer memorabilia.

The Gileses dined with Arnie and Winnie on numerous occasions, but one of Howdy's favorite memories was the morning when Arnie and Winnie called him at 6:30 on his birthday. Hoping to waken him from a sound sleep to wish him "Happy Birthday," they were amazed to find him up and about. He had been awake since 5:45, organizing his collection of more than 100 Arnold Palmer videos.

Dr. Brad Bastow
1995 Golf Nut of the Year
When you're the only person in the state of Michigan—perhaps the entire U.S.—who has a $36,000 Optromics "Par-T-Golf" golf simulator in your home, you're definitely "nuts." Meet Brad Bastow, golf nut extraordinaire.

"I have a compulsive passion for doing things," he says. "And golf is one of my true passions. I work 80 to 100 hours a week as a cardiologist. But the rest of the time I get everything I can to revolve around golf."

This is a man whose secretary arranges "foursomes" for him and his friends each week during the winter at his home on the simulator. They arrive dutifully at his home for their appointed tee times on "The Incredible Golf Machine," as they call it.

Bastow can't seem to get enough golf, even when it's "high-tech" golf. He averages four to five 18-hole rounds a week. Anyone playing the simulator for the first time must sign the "Wall of Fame" and enter their name in his journal. Both the wall and the journal feature names of people from around the world, including several touring pros. When they play the simulator for the first time, Brad plays them for a signed dollar bill. Whenever he wins a bet, he keeps the signed bills in his "Rolodex of Shame."

There are three mirrors installed in the "Golf Room" just in case anyone playing on the simulator wants to do a quick swing plane check.

"I beat Nicklaus at Cyber Golf. I guess it's stretching it to say that I once played golf with Jack, isn't it?" says Brad.

And just in case you think he's not serious about improving his game, check this: he placed classified ads in both the *Kalamazoo Gazette* and the Benton Harbor *Herald-Palladium*, seeking a live-in golf pro to be hired on a full-time basis throughout the winter of 1994-95. Brad's goal? To become a scratch golfer. He interviewed twelve candidates and ultimately signed one of them, a David Leadbetter disciple, to an employment contract. The contract called for 120 hours of golf lessons throughout the winter.

Concerned that the golf professional might not be able to teach him effectively using only the golf simulator, Brad decided to purchase a condominium at The Vineyards, a private 36-hole country club in Naples, FL He and his instructor then made several trips to Florida throughout the winter months, practicing and playing 36 holes everyday.

One of his Florida trips in 1994 coincided with his wife's birthday—and he didn't even invite her along. Yikes. And then, in 1995, he repeated the same mistake, leaving her at home with the kids again. Apparently, he decided he couldn't be distracted from his mission. Nonetheless, despite this commitment to improvement, his handicap remained at 13.9. So he decided to drop the Leadbetter Method and not renew his contract with the pro. Now he's back to tearing golf articles out of golf magazines and filing them by category (Driving, Putting, Chipping, etc.).

Rob Gillette
1996 Golf Nut of the Year

Despite being a top executive for the Marriott Corporation, Rob Gillette always seemed to find time to be at all of golf's major championships. Rob is the Founder of the Ben Crenshaw Fan Club, "Ben's Battalion," and is naturally a big Crenshaw supporter. So it stands to reason that anytime he can weave his business responsibilities together with his passion for golf, he will find a way to do it. His brother has nicknamed him, "The Forrest Gump of Golf."

His efforts, on occasion, were apparently so transparent that he was actually accused by his boss of arranging his business trips around PGA Tour events. He, of course, denied it. What's a "nut" to do? Coincidentally, in 1995 alone he attended The Masters, U.S. Open, PGA Championship, Ryder Cup, and U.S. Senior Open.

And then there was the time that he drove from Germantown to Rochester, NY to watch the 1995 Ryder Cup. He arrived at 3:00 a.m. and, unable to find the home of a friend with whom he would be staying, slept in his car outside the gate of Oak Hill Country Club.

Sometimes Gillette's devotion borders on the insane. In 1996 he decided at the last moment to go to the PGA Championship and take his young sons with him, despite not having airline tickets, hotel reservations, tournament tickets, or permission from his wife.

In 1995 Rob drove from Maryland to Augusta, GA to attend The Masters. During a weak moment he promised his Sunday Masters badge to a friend so his friend could witness his first golf tournament. Rob then drove home to Maryland on Saturday, and watched the final round of The Masters from his living room. Unfortunately for Rob, it was the year of Crenshaw's emotional victory, and he had to watch the final round on television. Adding further insult, he saw his friend on national television, on the 18th tee, with his ticket. And if that weren't enough punishment, Rob received 35 congratulatory phone calls the day after the 1995 Masters (one from Australia), with most saying, "I saw you on TV Sunday on the 18th hole."

And then who could forget the Isleworth Pro-Am on his wife's 30th birthday. Certainly not his wife. That morning at breakfast he gave her a tennis bracelet and had his cousin's aunt and uncle entertain her for the day while he played in the Pro-Am and stayed for the dinner, which lasted until 10 p.m. Knowing he was in big trouble back at the homestead, he talked Payne Stewart into calling Debbie from the Pro-Am to wish her a happy birthday.

But any golf nut worth his stripes will tell you it was all worth it. After all, at his dinner table were Ben Crenshaw, Fred Couples, and Joe Gibbs, the president of The Golf Channel.

Tom Jewell
1997 Golf Nut of the Year

In 1985 Tom Jewell hurt his back and was told by his doctor to stay in bed for three weeks. During the second week a friend called with an invitation to play Augusta National. This being the first time he had been invited to the world-famous course, Tom immediately called his doctor to ask him if he would be well enough to play. The doctor replied that he must stay flat on his back for another 10 days, and then it would be safe for him to go. "Needless to say," Jewell said, "I hardly moved for 10 days, made my first trip to Augusta National and played the course for the first time. As it turned out, it was on my 55th birthday."

But Tom's addiction didn't start in 1985. On April 8, 1956, Tom played golf at Locust Hill Country Club in Rochester, NY. I guess that isn't all that unusual. But then there was snow on the ground. The temperature was 31 degrees. And his newlywed bride walked with him all 18 holes but didn't play. It was the first day of their honeymoon.

Tom seems to have an affinity for cold weather golf. Well, at least he used to. Before retiring to Florida he played golf every New Year's Day at 8 a.m., regardless of the weather, at his home club, Echo Lake Country Club in New Jersey. One year the wind chill factor was minus 20 degrees.

A senior executive for J.C. Penney, Tom's passion for golf paid off in a big way a few years ago when he was named the Tournament Director of the J.C. Penney Classic PGA/LPGA Tour event. Every Monday morning, partly because he is one of the nicest people you will ever meet, and partly to promote his tournament, Tom would send a handwritten letter of congratulations to the winners of the past week's PGA, LPGA, and Senior PGA tour events.

Unable to get enough of the game he loves, Tom does a lot of charitable and volunteer work in the Florida area, mostly revolving around golf activities for youngsters. His charitable activities didn't go unnoticed. In 1994 he was named North Florida PGA and West Central Chapter Amateur of the Year for his service to the community through golf volunteerism.

Wendi Keene
1998 Golf Nut of the Year

Wendi Keene was the first woman to win the coveted Golf Nut of the Year title, and boy did she earn it! This is a person who didn't pick up a golf club until she was 38 years old. Her reason for doing it? "Because I knew I could and should play this mysterious game which beholds 'The Secret.'"

She was a fast learner too, reducing her handicap to 17 within two years. And she did it her way. Wendi was more than a little uptight about being a beginner, so she set up an indoor driving range in her garage and used it every night for the first six months before ever venturing out onto a real golf course. She would even go so far as to rent a video camera for her indoor practice sessions. But after practicing in her garage for four months, she realized that she needed professional help (no kidding!).

Actually, she found a golf professional who agreed to analyze her swing via video, and she began sending him the video of her indoor practice sessions.

Then, like a bolt out of the blue, she got the bright idea to start over.

After playing golf right-handed for seven years, she decided to switch to left-handed. She's now been playing left-handed for more than seven years, is a 14-handicapper, and has shot as low as 76. She still keeps a right-handed handicap, which is 19. Now that's nuts. But it does have its advantages. Wendi always carries a right-handed and a left-handed driver in her bag, along with two other right-handed clubs, just in case the opportunity arises to demonstrate her ambidexterity.

Wendi has always had a knack for the unusual. She used to pick up range balls in return for golf privileges. Then she would pay the local kids 50 cents each to pick up the balls in the traps and other difficult areas. She even has her own private practice area at the back of the driving range. It has an area for hitting full shots, as well as a putting, chipping, and pitching area. She closes the range down at least once a week at her home course, Sedona Golf Resort, in Sedona, AZ.

Wendi is fond of saying that she has "no tolerance for golfers who aren't sincere about the game." And on one occasion she proved that she meant business. She proposed divorce to her ex-husband while standing near the 18th green during the final round of an LPGA tournament in Santa Barbara. Apparently, he lacked the sincerity necessary to match this golf nut's passion for the game.

Nobby Orens
1999 Golf Nut of the Year

On July 20, 1999, Nobby Orens entered the Guinness Book of World Records by playing 18 holes of golf in London, New York, and Los Angeles. In a single day. Honest.

He teed off at 4:58 a.m. at Stockley Park Golf Course in London, England then took The Concorde to New York, arriving at 9:20 a.m. There he had a helicopter waiting to take him to Clearview Golf Course where he played 18 holes in 1 hour and 5 minutes. He then helicoptered back to the airport where he took a noon nonstop flight to Los Angeles. Upon arriving in Los Angeles, another helicopter was waiting to take him to Braemar Country Club, where he played his third 18-hole round of the day, finishing at 5:00 p.m.

"I had time for at least another nine," quipped Nobby.

While it might sound strange, this sort of behavior is sort of normal for Orens. In 1999 he played 134 rounds of golf on 36 different courses in 27 different cities, five states, six countries, and two continents. In 1998 he played 150 rounds in 41 cities, seven states, and 14 countries. In 1998 he flew a total of 38,445 miles during one 6-month period just to play golf.

For example, there was this trip to Hawaii from New York. On June 18, 1998 he played 18 holes of golf in New York, and 18 holes in Honolulu. He teed off at 5:10 a.m. in New York and played his first round, finishing at 6:40 a.m. He then flew to Honolulu, connecting through Los Angeles. In Honolulu he chartered a helicopter to take him to the first tee of the Ko Olina golf course, teeing off at 5:05 p.m. and finishing at 7:15 p.m. He flew home the next morning.

It must be addictive, because on September 22, 1998 he flew to Auckland, New Zealand, leaving at 10:30 a.m. and arriving at 6 a.m. on September 24. He went directly to Gulf Harbor Country Club and played 18 holes. He then boarded a return flight to Los Angeles, leaving Auckland at 6:00 p.m. He arrived in Los Angeles at 11:00 a.m. on September 24th, drove to his home club and played 18 more holes.

This ended the 13,008 mile journey on which he had played 18 holes in Auckland and 18 holes in Los Angeles in the same day. The following day, September 25, he flew to Maui, Hawaii to play in a 100-hole golf tournament.

Whew!

So, is there a point to all this? We're not sure. But we think it might have something to do with the way he thinks. His front doormat reads, "A golfer and a normal person live here."

Nobby immerses himself in whatever he is doing, and lately that's been golf. So he has a TV remote in the shape of a golf hole, complete with sand traps and a green with a flag. When first turned on, the remote says "Fore," and you hear the ball dropping into a cup, followed by cheers.

When you change channels it makes a sound like a golf club hitting a ball. And his golf "by the numbers" is pretty impressive too. He has played two or more rounds in a single day 30 times in his career. His fastest round of golf is one hour five minutes. He has played more than 1,000 rounds, and in 75 golf tournaments since 1993.

"I also flew up to Alaska (in 1998) to play for 24 hours," Orens reminds us. "But was given misinformation and had to quit at midnight so I only got in 200 holes."

And he has every score of every round he's ever played since starting golf in September 1993. He keeps statistics on average score for the month, and year-to-date, as well as total rounds, fairways, greens, and putts.

Mike Noyes
2000 Golf Nut of the Year

In 2000, Mike Noyes was a busy guy. So busy that he put up with a nagging hernia all year long. Well, truth be told, he didn't want to suffer the downtime of a hernia operation and miss all of that golf he plays. He also had quintuple heart bypass surgery, but that didn't stop him either.

On Tuesday, February 29, 2000, he went into the hospital for the surgery; was back home, chipping and putting on his backyard putting green the following Tuesday, and played 18 holes just 1 1/2 months after the bypass surgery. He also practiced chipping and putting in his backyard every day since his surgery. You would think, after picking up his first golf club at age 4 and playing his first round of golf at age 8, approximately 53 years ago, Mike could give it a rest at least long enough to get healthy. But telling a golf nut he can't play golf is kind of like telling a drug addict to go "cold turkey." It just ain't gonna happen, at least not without a fight.

One of Mike's greatest loves is collecting golf memorabilia. He has acquired 2,145 golf books over his 53-year golf career, and to date he has spent more than $4,000 to purchase over 250 golf items on eBay. In 1999 he purchased a collection of Bob Hope Tournament jewelry for $1,500 that has been shown at the Ralph W. Miller Golf Library in California.

His collection of more than 100 yards of golf ties are the only ties he wears to work, and his 83 golf shirts, sweaters, and jackets don't seem excessive at all to him. Some of his 70-plus hickory golf clubs are pre-1800 vintage. And he has so many golf collectibles he had to rent a storage unit to hold it all. He still can't park his car in his garage due to golf paraphernalia.

In an all-out effort to win the 2000 Golf Nut of the Year title, Mike took his hernia, his bad knee, his bad back, and his quintuple bypassed heart on a sensory deprivation death march that began on Thursday, December 28, 2000, and ended, thankfully, 24 hours later. The effort included hitting 200 balls, playing 18 holes at Mile Square Golf Course, driving to D.L. Baker Golf Course, practicing putting and then playing 18 holes of night golf.

Upon arriving home at 10:45 p.m., he spent the next 6 1/2 hours putting and chipping under the Christmas lights that adorn his beloved Dry Creek Golf Club backyard course. He putted cross-handed, with eyes open and closed, and used several different putters including an original Wilson 8802, T.P. Mills, Schenectady, Dandy, and SeeMore putter. To cap off this marathon, he drove to his home club, Meadowlark Golf Club, and hit 32 balls, had breakfast and played nine more holes. Then he went to work.

To finish off the year, he hit a shot with his Cleveland Tour Action 60-degree sand wedge just prior to midnight on December 31, 2000, that stayed in the air until after midnight, thus hitting a shot from the Second Millennium into the Third Millennium. 1,000 points.

All in a career's work as a Golf Nut, Noyes insists modestly.

Ivan Morris
2001 Golf Nut of the Year

What would you do if your wife was about to give birth to your second child right in the middle of the biggest golf tournament of the year? Induce labor, of course.

Well, that's just exactly what Irishman Ivan Morris did two weeks before the 1980 Interprovincial Championships at Royal County Down. And then he went on to win the championship. Sounds like it was a very wise decision. It also earned him a thousand Nut points.

But the real question is why would his lovely wife, Marie, agree to such a preposterous proposition? Maybe she's nuts too. As it turned out, it was a very difficult delivery, but ended well as they added a son, David, to the family.

"I promised Marie a really good holiday in 1981 to make up for all the suffering and discomfort that David and I had put her through."

So where did he take her? Augusta, GA, to see The Masters. Oh, and did I mention that he had the family pose for a photo with the trophy – a very large cup – and little David was placed comfortably inside the cup for the photo op. Go nuts.

Such is the life of the first non-American golf nut to win the Golf Nut of the Year title. Yes, Ivan is nuts. He even wrote a book about his life, entitled *Only Golf Spoken Here*. And as if that weren't enough, he also collaborated with legendary Irish caddie John O'Reilly to produce a book entitled *The Life of O'Reilly*.

Ivan's "holiday" to The Masters wasn't quite the holiday that he had promised the lovely Marie. They arrived in Augusta without tickets to the event, which any self-respecting golf nut will tell you is foolhardy. It's the toughest ticket in all of sports. However, it didn't seem to pose a problem for Ivan. Before he was through casting his spell, he had garnered enough tickets for himself, Marie and a couple of friends who had come along on the trip.

But my favorite story about Ivan is the ten-year "golf discussion" he engaged in with a Canadian golfer he met by chance during a round of golf. Over the next ten years, he and his newfound golf buddy exchanged over 900 audiotapes of golf discussion that totaled nearly 1,500 hours of conversation, discussing and arguing over nearly every golf subject imaginable. Now that's nuts! It was also worth 1,900 Nut points.

Ivan might have lost a little distance on his drives over the years, but he hasn't lost any of his passion for the game. On December 30, 2001, just two days before he was notified that he had won the Golf Nut of the Year title, Ivan went to the driving range at his home club, only to find that it was closed. Determined to get in a little practice, he found an empty range basket and picked up about 100 muddy balls from the range. After a little more searching, he discovered a barrel full of rainwater near the range, broke through the ice and washed the balls with his bare hands, and hit the balls back out into the range. After his hands thawed, of course. You've got to be committed.

Ivan will always have the distinction of being the first international winner of the coveted Golf Nut of the Year title, and we're proud that it went to someone with his passion and love for the game.

Corbin Cherry
A Living Example To Us All
Corbin has the distinction of having qualified for both the U.S. Senior Open and the U.S. Senior Amateur during his long and successful amateur career.

This takes on monumental significance when you consider he has also won the National Amputee Championship seven times. Yes, Corbin Cherry is an amputee. And Corbin is a great golfer.

More than 30 years ago, Mr. Cherry made a sacrifice that at the time he wasn't prepared to make. But with grace and dignity he has used his sacrifice to become an icon for other Vietnam veterans who came home wounded from the war. Despite losing his right leg below the knee when a land mine detonated beneath him in a rice field, Corbin Cherry made good on his promise to himself to become the best that he could be at the game he loved so much. And for more than 30 years now, he has become good enough to beat the best in the game.

You see, Cherry was an army chaplain. The mine detonated beneath him when he was helping evacuate injured soldiers. When the sergeant arrived to carry him away. Well.................here are Cherry's words:

"The explosion of the land mine had blown me down into a ravine. I was wounded and lying there in the jungle and I didn't know how I'd be able to play golf again. I applied a tourniquet with the bootstrap from my left leg. The sergeant was crying as he looked at me and asked if I was OK.

"I said, 'Sarge, how am I going to be able to play golf on one leg?'"

"He said, 'What?'"

Cherry repeated himself.

"Excuse me, Chaplain," the sergeant said, "but you're one crazy sumbitch."

Cherry lived to play golf another day. His story is about as heroic as it gets in our little society. But it, too, is nuts.

Cherry chuckles when talking about what he calls his "nutdom."

"Golf has been so good to me," he says. "I played 173 rounds of golf in 2001. I am 65 years old. I play better now than I ever played. I have educated myself more about the game and I know its true values.

"Ron Garland? I must say I am truly amused by him. He likes the game almost in the same stratosphere as I do. And he's one of the most articulate people in golf."

And, Corbin, you are without question the most inspirational person in golf.

Those are our legends; the golf nuts who have gone on to greatness in one form or another. I invite you to read more about them on our website (www.golfnuts.com).

9th Hole

"IT'S GOLF OR ME!"

Golf nuts come in all types, and they manifest their "commitment" to golf in a variety of ways. I've learned this firsthand, because I'm pretty sure I've "scored points" in every way possible.

This chapter is about the centuries-old "battle of the sexes." One of my favorite stories in the marriage category relates to a "Dear Abby" column I read several years ago. It's still fresh in my mind because it clearly demonstrates the dilemma faced by the spouses of "golf nuts" anywhere in the world. Here is the full text of that exchange:

"Dear Abby,

My fiancé and I recently moved from New York to Florida. "Morey" and I are both divorced and look forward to having someone to share our lives with. He has friends and relatives here, whereas I have no one. Part of the reason he moved to Florida is because he loves to play golf. At first, he golfed either on Saturday or Sunday. However, lately he's been golfing on both days. He's gone from four to six hours at a crack, and when he gets home, he's usually too tired to do anything because he got up so early. We've had some serious talks about his golfing, and he made it clear that he "loves" the sport, and if I become too resentful of his golfing, we will have problems. We both work full time during the week, and I think I'm entitled to have him all to myself one day a week. While he plays golf, I stay home with my children (from a previous marriage) and do laundry and cleaning. Am I being selfish and inconsiderate, or is he?"

Abby's reply was profound. She replied,

"Dear Golf Widow:

Labeling him - or you - 'selfish and inconsiderate' won't solve anything. He warned you that if you became too resentful of his golf game, you'd have problems. Believe him. If you want Morey in your life, cultivate a few friends and find something to do while he's playing golf. Don't nag and don't sulk. And never give a golfer an ultimatum unless you're prepared to lose."

Profound indeed.

I've already chronicled some of my earlier insanity as it relates to my marriage, and all I have to say in my defense is that given the opportunity to rewrite history on that score I wouldn't. I'm sorry, but I can't help myself. When I said to Judy, "I loved golf before I loved you, don't ever make me choose," I meant it. It doesn't mean that I love golf more than I love her; it means that if she loves me she won't ask me to give up something that I loved before I met her. Make sense? Well, it does to me. And apparently she understood what I meant, too. At least so far.

And then there's the case of Marshall Gleason, Nut #0008. Deeply in love with a fellow "golf nut" (not the "Registered" kind), the two lovebirds decided to recite their wedding vows at one of the most breathtaking backdrops in the world—behind the third tee at Mauna Kea, on the big island of Hawaii—a place where hundreds of couples have done the same. There's a cute little wedding arch that is only a few yards behind the championship tee of this unbelievable golf hole that overlooks a gorgeous rock cove that forms the carry over a 200-yard expanse of the Pacific Ocean.

Marshall and Nancy were married amid this spectacular scenery, only to return three years later to try to "save" their marriage. When the two reached the third tee at Mauna Kea and teed off, little did they know what awaited them on the green. Upon reaching the green, they looked at each other and said, "Well, should we end it here?" The answer was "Yes," and then they finished the round. How romantic.

There is, however, a happy ending to this story. Marshall and Nancy are at least still in love with golf. And from time to time they tee it up together. In 2002, in fact, Nancy was going to caddie for Marshall in the Oregon Amateur at Bandon Dunes until he spoiled everything with emergency bypass surgery. What a pair(ing).

But in my opinion David McMillin (#0328) takes the cake for blind devotion—to the Greater Greensboro Open, that is. You see, his wife went into labor during the middle of the tournament (the nerve!) and David dutifully took her to the hospital. That's when the plot thickened. But rather than me telling you, let's hear it straight from David. Here's a letter I received from him describing the eventful weekend:

"Dear Head Nut,

I would be proud to become an "official" golf nut through the Golf Nuts Society. As evidence of my sincerity, I'd like to relate a recent story. My wife, Sheila, delivered our first-born (Heather Nicole) on April 3rd of this year. The baby was two weeks overdue, so labor had to be induced. It worked out perfectly because the hospital had ESPN, which my home doesn't, and I was able to watch the Greater Greensboro Open during labor. The baby was delivered by a C-Section, but fortunately did not arrive until the coverage was over. As luck would have it, I was able to watch the Saturday and Sunday rounds while my wife recuperated in the hospital."

Sincerely,

David Lee McMillin

Vincent, Alabama

Now that's devotion.

And let's not forget the legendary performance of Steve Thorwald, Nut #0476.

Scheduled to be married one sunny Saturday afternoon, he and his future father-in-law decided to get in a quick 18 before the wedding. Well, the pace of play wasn't what they had hoped it would be— and they weren't about to quit the round over a mere wedding—so they finished the round, rushed to the parking lot and grabbed their tuxedos. Running late, they sprinted back into the locker room and changed into the tuxedos without a shower. They made a mad dash for the wedding chapel, arriving only minutes before the ceremony began.

Not content with this "close call," Steve unintentionally put his new bride through the acid test. So blinded by his love of golf, and finding himself in Hawaii, he did what came naturally. On the first day of the honeymoon he teedoff at 7:32 a.m. and played 36 holes of golf. He woke up the next morning to find that he hadn't been killed in his sleep, so he teed it up for another 36 holes. That went so well, he did it again the next day. Thirty-six holes a day—without his newlywed bride—the first three days of his honeymoon. That's just downright unbelievable. Oh, did I mention—the marriage didn't last.

"In retrospect, I must admit that my love for the game may have taken precedence over familial duties once or thrice," Thorwald says. "I really thought my former wife loved the game because she paid my entry fee to a tournament for a wedding present. We played a few times on our honeymoon and a few times after that. But then the cheering stopped."

Steve is now remarried to Trina Thorwald, Registered Golf Nut #2861. Some marriages are made in heaven. "My lovely wife Trina loves the game as much as I do," Thorwald adds. "In fact our vacation this year is a trip to Bandon Dunes (Oregon) to meet GNS friends and play the already legendary Dunes courses. I would say our love for each other has grown partly because of golf, not in spite of it."

Oh, and we mustn't forget Luis Sanchez (#0827). His regular foursome has been faithful to each other through 18 girlfriends, three fiancées, and three divorces. For that I have awarded him 1,018 points.

Here, in his words, is his story: "This foursome was assembled in the early '80s from a group of grocery store employees. We had been a foursome long before any girlfriends or wives. We continued to play, much to the annoyance of the wives and girlfriends. Every Thursday was our scheduled day of worship. It was 18 or 36 holes in the morning, then golf league in the afternoon. We all ran exceptional stores but our time off was ours and we chose to play golf.

"Jamie, one of the foursome, came home one Thursday to find his home vacant, except for the stack of past due bills. This did not get much reaction, the biggest reaction was upon finding his spare set of irons impaled in the walls of the house—nine irons, nine holes. His putter was in the backyard, it had been thrown through the arcadia window. His two woods had been impaled in the front and back doors. Divorce #1.

"Tony's game was just beginning to blossom when misfortune struck him down. His wife sold his clubs at a garage sale for $50; clubs, bags, balls, shoes, shirts, hats, etc. He was left with no other alternative but to replace his then 20-year-old clubs with the newest Ping irons on the market. Misfortune struck again as 'they were stolen from his ex-wife's car while at church.' Magically, they reappeared in a photo, being played with by her brother in North Dakota. Divorce #2.

"Jack was a devout golfer who sacrificed his soul to play golf. I know this because how can you explain playing in an Arizona monsoon and shooting a career round. His wife left him when she found their oldest son taking divots from the living room carpet to 'be like daddy.' He quietly began dating the cart girl at our neighborhood course. They are still married to this day.

"Jack and I would take golf trips to Tucson, Palm Springs, or Flagstaff and still make it home for golf league. His girlfriend knew his affliction before they began dating so she knew what she was getting into beforehand.

"I had been engaged to my high school sweetheart when upon finally being given the question 'Me or golf' the decision was easy. She was last heard from dating a nongolfing wimp who volunteered to caddie at our 20-year reunion just to meet some of us that had the backbone that he did not possess."

Bravo, Luis.

Tom Jewell (#0175) played golf on his honeymoon in 25 degree temperatures and bitter cold wind with his newlywed bride at his side. This earned him 250 points. Jewell's own words:

"Lavon and I were married on April 7, 1956 in Kalamazoo, MI. We drove to Niagara Falls that night and stayed at—are you ready—'The Honeymoon Motel.' Then it was on to Rochester the next day. I grew up in Rochester and caddied at Oak Hill C.C. and played at public courses. At age 15 Mom and Dad joined Locust Hill C.C.. I loved Locust Hill—a great track where the LPGA played every year. I wanted Lavon to see the course I grew up on. So, carrying my golf bag, no carts in 1956, we walked 18 holes, me playing, Lavon watching. It was in the mid-20s with snow on the ground. Crazy!!!! No one else played that day."

Now, just in case you think we're the only ones around here who are nuts, take a look at these Nuts:

Bob Valentine (#0010) - Proposed to his girlfriend one Saturday when she refused to let him play golf. She relented and allowed him to play, but the marriage didn't last. 300 points.

Marty Price (#0038) - Gave his fiancée three weekend dates to choose from for their impending wedding. All the other weekends were taken up with golf tournaments. 300 points.

Paul Renberg (#0135) - He told his newlywed bride that he played golf on Saturdays, and that golf "takes about eight hours to play." She found out two years later from one of Paul's friends, that golf only takes four hours to play. 180 points.

Gene Norene (#0189) - Was playing golf in a snowstorm in Ithaca, NY. when his second son was born in Wisconsin. 1,000 points.

Tom Jensen (#0245) - Delayed his honeymoon because he unexpectedly made the finals of a match play golf tournament. Still believes that he would have won if his newlywed bride had done a better job of caddying. 500 points.

Tracy Sergeant (#0734) - Scheduled his wedding ceremony for Saturday morning so he could play in a golf tournament that afternoon, with his newlywed bride as his caddie. The reception had to be delayed until two weeks later so as not to interfere with his golf tournament schedule. It was held at his home club. 500 points.

Thaddeus Czerniak (#1027) - His ex-wife gave him a list of 10 reasons she was divorcing him. The third item on the list was that he got grass in the trunk of her car from his golf shoes. 300 points.

Doug Wiese (#1258) - Spent two consecutive Mother's Day weekends at Troon Golf Club in Scottsdale, AZ leaving his wife, mother, and son behind in rainy Oregon. Mother's Day was also his mother's birthday. She is a partner in a restaurant in Oregon with him. She stayed behind to run the restaurant. Ouch! 1,000 points.

Dr. Mark Mavis (#2390) - Took his wife on a one-day trip to the Bahamas for her birthday and played golf all day long with a buddy, which included a two-hour "monsoon delay." 300 points.

As stories like these continue to flood into the world headquarters of the Golf Nuts Society it has crossed my mind that it's a miracle that any of these people have remained married (including me).

Golf and marriage: The irresistible force meets the immovable object. And the irresistible force wins. Or as Luis Sanchez nicely sums it up: "I am married to a marvelous woman who planned our reception at the golf course we first played together, a honeymoon in the Bahamas with tee times every day we were there and anniversaries at the golf resort where we first fell in love, along the first fairway of Gold Canyon in Arizona. I may not know her bust size but I can tell you her USGA handicap."

Go nuts.

"Sorry, gotta run to an important appointment."

10th Hole

WHAT, ME WORK?

If you were to ask any self-respecting golf nut whether he would rather work or play golf, he might look at you as though you had some strange and highly contagious virus, and bolt for the door. Of course we would rather play golf than work. What kind of question is that?

Unfortunately, most golf nuts have to go to work just like normal people do. Unless you're Joe Malay. Then it's a real problem. You remember Joe. He's the guy who retired out of high school because work would have a negative effect on his golf.

"I'm independently happy," Joe likes to say.

Anyway, Joe Malay notwithstanding, work is always getting in the way of our golf.

I remember there was a time when the company I was working for had scheduled a two-day training session in Santa Cruz, CA, just a 9-iron down the street from Pasatiempo, one of the greatest golf courses in America. And to make matters worse, they scheduled no free time for "personal business" during the business day. And then, showing absolutely no sensitivity to my needs whatsoever, they scheduled the training from 8 a.m. to 5 p.m. each of the two days, when sunrise was 6:30 and sunset was 6:15.

To complicate things even further, we were required to be at dinner by

7:00. This was going to take some creative thought, followed by precise execution, but here was the plan I hatched. I played the front nine the first evening, bolting the training session as soon as it ended, and teed off at 5:15. I finished in exactly one hour, holing out in the gathering gloom. I drove back to the hotel in plenty of time for dinner. The next morning I got up early and teed off on the back nine at 6:30. It was totally dark outside. I finished in less than an hour. I even made it back in time to scarf down a quick breakfast before the meeting began. (You've got to be committed.)

Then there was the time, in 1989, when I was in San Jose on a business trip during the first two rounds of The Masters. I was already frustrated about having to be out of town during the season's first major, when I arrived at my hotel that evening to find out that they didn't carry the USA Network. I had been looking forward to going back to my hotel room at the end of the day, ordering a pizza, and watching the reruns of the first round. This meant that my plans had turned to ashes, so I refused to check into the hotel until I had investigated my alternatives.

I drove to seven different hotels and called four others, trying to find one that carried the USA Network. Sadly, none did, so I reluctantly checked into the hotel and asked the concierge to find a restaurant or bar that carried the telecast. He found a place called "Mountain Mike's Pizza" in another city, 15 miles away, but when I arrived, "Mountain Mike" couldn't get the broadcast to come in. Dejected and defeated, I returned to the hotel, called home, and asked my wife to tape the telecast for me so I could watch it when I returned home.

And how could I ever forget that wonderful three-day business trip to Boise back in 1990, when I made a grand total of three sales calls and played 81 holes of golf. Ah, the good old days. I was so worn out from the grueling trip to Boise that I decided I needed a little R&R. So Judy and I flew to Carefree, AZ, where we drove 400 miles around the state while I played 171 holes of golf in seven days. Now that's what I call a relaxing getaway from the daily grind. I came back refreshed and ready to get back to work.

As I look back over the stories I've heard through the years, one of my all-time favorites was about Craig Stainbrook, Nut #0005, of Portland, OR. Craig, now a trademark and patent attorney in Santa Rosa, CA, was always one of those guys who gave one hundred percent to anything he did. When he decided that he wanted to learn to play golf, he sought out the legendary teaching pro Bob Duden to give him lessons.

"Duden was a great teacher for me," Stainbrook recalls. "I had unlimited access and he could answer any question. I worked with him for a month or so and started to play in the low 70s and snuck in a few rounds in the 60s. That's when it clicked that I should play the game seriously. Naturally, life goes to hell in a handbasket once you get serious about the harshest of mistresses. And so it goes."

Craig went on to have a brilliant amateur career in Oregon, followed by a stint as a golf professional, before a shoulder injury sidelined him.

But that's not why I tell you about Craig. This chapter is about golf and work, and while what Craig did during his first six months in the game seems a lot more like work than golf to a golf nut like me, he has an even more compelling story to tell.

When Craig was just taking up the game he worked as a driving range attendant at the venerable Eastmoreland Municipal Golf Course in Portland. One of his jobs was to pick up all of the balls on the range at the end of the day. Eastmoreland is a lighted facility, and stayed open until 9 p.m. Then it was Craig's job to "pick up the range." Now, when somebody tells me that they "picked up the range," I envision them getting into one of those caged vehicles—you know, the ones that we all aim at as soon as they pull out onto the range—and drive around to pick up the balls.

Not Craig's idea at all. On more than one occasion he would grab his trusty 7-iron and start swinging for the fences. He would start at the front of the range and hit the balls toward the back of the range, and when he had hit them all to the back fence, then he would fire up the range mobile. I can't even imagine how many balls he must have hit on those evenings, but it had to be in the thousands. And some of them had to be hit more than once. All these years later, I still have this image in my mind of a solitary figure—alone with his thoughts, dreams, and aspirations—standing in the middle of a deserted driving range surrounded by thousands of golf balls.

"This was actually a really wonderful time in my life," Stainbrook says now. "I was about a year or so into playing the game seriously. I'd never played any competitive golf and needed a lot of time with a club in my hands. I was coming to the game so late that I had no time to waste before I began to waste life. So I got a job at Eastmoreland and worked late at night so I could play during the day.

"The job entailed picking up the range at night and then staying up the entire night to watch the clubhouse and generally discourage vandalism and burglary. There seemed to be an understanding that anyone who did this job actually fell asleep on the soft seats in the coffee shop booths in the early morning hours and I was no exception.

"In my first hours on the job between about 10 p.m. and 1 a.m. we picked up the range. I don't think I was unique in spending a little, if not a lot of time hitting balls into the back of the range. But I did make a point of turning the job into a practice session (how could one not do so?). In any event, it was a bit too cumbersome to take a variety of clubs out to the grass. So either before or after picking up the range generally, I kept a spot littered with balls so I could hit a selected club roughly the distance to the end of the range and I whacked those balls until I was too tired to continue. Then I picked up the rest of the range. No big deal, really. Any golf nut would do the same."

Beautiful. The floodlights carving out a rectangular slice of heaven for a lone golf nut as darkness surrounds him. Craig had his own Field of Dreams. Cool.

Marshall Gleason is another great story. He decided that it was time for a little vacation, so he entered the North & South Invitational at the Pinehurst Resort in North Carolina. Nothing like a world-class golf tournament on one of the greatest golf courses in the world to get your mind off work for a few days. Little did Gleason know what lay ahead.

Wanting to get away from the hustle and bustle of tournament headquarters at Pinehurst, Marshall opted to stay at the nearby Mid-Pines Resort. On the day of the first round, he warmed up at the Mid-Pines driving range and then drove the short distance to Pinehurst, arriving just ten minutes prior to his tee time. This would leave him plenty of time to hit a few putts and then tee off.

As he entered the parking lot, he was surprised to find there were no parking spaces, so he sort of "created" a parking space by parking on a precarious side hill along the edge of the parking lot. He got out of his car, opened the trunk, dropped his keys into his golf bag, and was about to pull the bag out of the trunk when a car pulled out of a nearby parking spot.

He quickly decided to move his car, slammed the trunk, closed the door, jumped into the front seat of the car, and reached for the ignition.

No keys. They were in the trunk. In his golf bag. Oops.

Oh, my God! I tee off in the North & South Invitational in 10 minutes! he thought. What am I going to do?

A bit of quick thinking sent him into the pro shop where he told them of his predicament. He asked if they had a crowbar, and they quickly found one in the green superintendent's shop. Marshall returned to his car and tried to pop the lock on the trunk. No luck. So he did the same thing that any self-respecting golf nut would in a similar situation: he peeled back the metal on the top of the trunk where it joined the left-rear bumper, reached in and rescued his clubs one at a time. He certainly handled it better than I would have. If I imagine myself in a similar situation, I have these visions of me angrily beating the living crap out of the top of that trunk—and then missing my tee time.

Not Marshall. The pro shop explained the unusual situation to the starter, and asked him to "buy a little time" for Marshall's group, which he did. But it was only about five minutes' worth of breathing room. When Marshall returned to the pro shop, both of his forearms were scratched and bleeding, but he had his clubs in his hands (we'll talk about the condition of the trunk in a minute). The pro gave him a sleeve of golf balls, a golf bag, a towel, a handful of tees, and told him to make a beeline for the first tee.

"I had no chance," Gleason said later. "Blood was streaming down both arms as I teed off, and by the end of the front nine the towel was a bloody mess! I shot 80, missed the cut, and went home."

Due to the condition of the rental car, Marshall made the decision to return it to Hertz at 4:00 a.m., when there would be no staff around, hoping to avoid any "additional charges," if you know what I mean. A few weeks later he received a letter from Hertz, notifying him that there would be an additional charge of $400 to "repair the damage to the trunk." To which Marshall replied, "What damage to the trunk? It was in perfectly good condition when I returned it." To which they replied a few weeks later, "Right, you owe us $400," which he promptly paid.

The Society's motto is, "If You're Not Registered, How Can You Be Committed?" Marshall Gleason was definitely committed to that round in Pinehurst (or at least he should have been "committed" shortly after it ended); and after you read a few of the following stories, you'll agree that they're right there with him.

Jim Gibbons (#0394) - Played in a golf tournament under an assumed name, fearing that he would otherwise be caught playing hooky by his boss. 500 points.

Bill Vanderveer (#0187) - Arrived at his club for a quick nine holes after work, but forgot his shoes, so he bought a new pair and teed off. 100 Points.

Daniel Cedusky (#0470) - Played 18 holes one day, then drove 1 1/2 hours to St. Paul, MN to catch a flight. Flight was delayed, so he got back in his car and drove around until he found a golf course, and played another 18 holes. Went back to the airport, and was the last passenger to board the flight before it departed. 180 points.

Steve Post (#0623) - Turned down a real estate appointment — giving the client to a fellow agent — so he could play golf. The agent made a $6,500 commission, Steve shot 41 and won $1.75. 175 points.

Scott Marten (#1004) - He and his playing partner arose at 3:00 a.m., jumped into a car with two other friends, and bummed a five-hour ride from Newport Beach to San Luis Obispo, CA, for an 8:51 tee time in a one-day golf tournament. After the tournament (and one too many cocktails), they hitched a ride to the airport where they rented a car, drove to Monterey Peninsula and rented a room. They arose the next morning, put on the same clothes they had worn the previous day, called in sick to their employer from a pay phone, and played Spanish Bay. After the round, they returned to the airport and flew home. 300 points.

Rick Steinfeld (#1081) - Flew around the world on a six-day business trip, lugging his golf clubs with him in the hope that he might have a chance to play at least one round. Unfortunately, he never got to hit a single shot. 306 points.

Scott Grimshaw (#1122) - On a vacation in Reno he stayed up until four in the morning gambling, but still made his 6:15 a.m. tee time. 215 points.

Ulda DeBernardi (#1955) - A flight attendant, she missed her flight assignment because she was playing in a ladies golf league and lost track of time. 200 points.

Mike Butler (#1988) - Played golf at Augusta National, leaving his wife and two children in Florida on family vacation. In order to play, he had to pretend to be the sales manager of his friend's company when the friend's sales manager had to cancel at the last minute. 1,000 points.

Ken Kellaney (#2020) - Had a new set of clubs shipped to his office at the bank where he worked so he could immediately go to the driving range upon their arrival. 200 points.

Chris Goodwin (#2272) - He and his partner, John Drake (#2271), struck it rich and built their own personal golf course (Red Tail Golf Club, St. Thomas, Ontario, Canada). Chris and John are the only members. 5,000 points.

"What a perfect day for a round of golf!"

11th Hole

THE HEAVY STUFF

"I don't think the heavy stuff's gonna come down for quite a while yet"
—**Bill Murray in** *Caddyshack*

If you haven't played golf in lousy weather, you're not a golf nut. Sorry, but those are the rules. The reason is these blasted four seasons that we have to deal with! If it were summer 12 months a year we wouldn't have to go out in bad weather, so don't blame us. We're just doing what comes naturally.

I've played golf in rain, snow, sleet, hail, wind, cold, and heat, and I'll be the first to admit it's much more enjoyable playing golf in perfect weather. It's not like I get up every morning and say, "Boy, I sure hope it snows today. I'd like to get out for a few holes!" No, it's just that we golf nuts want to play golf twelve months a year, and the weather refuses to cooperate.

I actually once played golf in a tornado; however, it wasn't part of the original plan. I got up one morning with every intention of playing 18 holes of golf, but it was nasty weather, to say the least. The skies were very dark, the clouds were hovering low over the land, it was raining, and the wind was blowing hard from the southwest (not a good sign.) I decided to drive over to the golf course to see if the weather was better over there. That's the way we golf nuts think. Ever the optimists.

When I arrived at the course, I was greeted with the same weather (what a surprise!). I pulled the clubs out of the trunk and thought, "It's not really that bad." When I teed off I was the only person on the golf course (duh!), but pretty soon I was having the round of my life. I was a six handicap at the time, and had never shot in the 60s. To be perfectly honest, I hadn't even shot under par more than a couple of times, but I started hitting the ball like a touring pro, and making every putt I looked at. The weather was still lousy, but the golf was unbelievable. It was just like the scene in *Caddyshack* where Carl Spackler (Bill Murray) was caddying for the priest in the pouring rain.

I birdied the ninth hole to shoot 31 on the front, and went into the pro shop to warm up a little before tackling the back nine. As I was standing there talking to the pro, a guy came into the shop, his eyes bugged out, and he was talking real fast. He said that he was heading west up on Mill Plain Boulevard when he saw a big black cloud coming in his direction. He didn't think much of it until he saw telephone poles being snapped off at the base. That's when he turned around and drove like a bat out of hell in our direction. He said he had pulled into the golf course just to find a building to duck into.

About that time we saw that black cloud emerge over the corner of the course, only a few hundred yards from the pro shop. It was moving along at a pretty good clip, and there was the roof of a house blowing around in it!

"You don't suppose that's a tornado, do you?" I asked anxiously.

"Looks like one to me," said the pro.

"Nah, I don't think so. We don't have tornadoes in the northwest."

Of course, my 31 on the front nine heavily influenced my comment. I waited in the pro shop for about 5 or 10 minutes, keeping a wary eye on the general area of the cloud, and finally said, "I'm going out. I've got my career round workin' here. Besides, I don't think it's a tornado."

I finished what did turn out to be my career round, shooting a 35 on the back for a smooth 66. When I came back into the pro shop, the pro told me that what we had seen was in fact a tornado, and that an elementary school and several cars had been destroyed in the two spots where it had touched down. I felt lucky. Very lucky. I think that was the first time that I heard someone say, "Garland, you're nuts!" You know, I think they were right.

Years later, when *Sports Illustrated* did a story on the Golf Nuts Society and mentioned the tornado incident, I received a letter from a man named George Roth in which he wrote, "I, too, have played golf in a tornado (the one that wiped out Newton Falls, Ohio) and other weather that kept the nonlunatics off the golf courses. I hereby submit my application for membership to join your distinguished society."

As I said, I'm not alone.

But sometimes a guy just has to say "enough!" That's what happened to me after my aforementioned Arizona vacation. After a week of perfect weather in Arizona, I played in the Eastmoreland Chapman tournament in Portland, OR. As is too often the case in Oregon, the golf tournament was played in a horrific downpour, which prompted me to announce to my partner Peter Moore: "I will never play golf in the rain again for the rest of my life." One week later, I was playing golf in the rain again. Like I said earlier, if the weather would just cooperate, this sort of thing wouldn't have to happen.

Just recently, the weather failed to cooperate again. I went out to the local muni to play my regular weekly game with a couple of other golf nuts this past March. What looked like a "passable" day turned ugly in a matter of minutes. Now when I say "passable," I mean it was about 40 degrees, no wind, and no rain. As I said, passable. The front nine was rather uneventful weatherwise, so we all decided to play the back nine. No sooner did we get out on the 10th fairway, than the snow came. I mean it was snowing hard. As we were playing, one of the guys casually slid over to me and said, "It's been quite a while since I played in a blizzard."

But all I could think about was that I had not driven over to the golf course in my four-wheel drive rig. Sitting in the parking lot instead was my totally-worthless-in-the-snow passenger car. And I live up this pretty steep hill. I'm not going to make it home, I thought. So after about three more holes of this nonsense, I announced to the guys that I was going home. They all looked at me like there was something wrong with me; like they didn't want to get near me for fear that it might be contagious. One of them, Vince Martinez (#2824), even questioned my manhood, if you know what I mean.

So when I got back home, I sent out an e-mail to the Nuts at large, asking them to weigh in on the subject, and to tell me whether I should charge #2824 with insubordination for questioning my manhood, or reward him with bonus points for finishing the round in the snow. Before I share with you some of their responses, I probably should tell you I rewrote the Rules of Golf. So now we Nuts have our own version of The Rules, and here is Rule 6-8:

"Rule 6-8. Discontinuance of Play - The player shall not discontinue play unless the player is quitting the game forever. Bad weather is not of itself a good reason for discontinuing play if one is a true golf nut. Bad weather shall be limited to earthquakes, blizzards, typhoons, hurricanes, acid rain, and nuclear fallout, and can be easily endured, especially if one is under par."

Well, needless to say, the feedback from the full membership wasn't exactly supportive of my position. Here is what they had to say:

"Reward him with nut points in direct proportion to the wind chill divided by the number of inches of snow on the ground." - Don Gardiner (#2139)

"He gets the points; you get some chains!" - Mike "GNOTY 2000" Noyes.

"I just have not gotten over the shock that our leader, THE HN, would set this type of example. The game was meant to be played in all types of weather ....once begun it must be completed." - Sandy Alexander (#2729) (Easy for you to say, #2729, you live in Arizona! - HN).

"I think you should look for a house that has year-round access." - Ron

Kulchak (#0532).

"Reward him. It takes major Hail Stones to finish in a blizzard." – Maxi Driver (#2790).

"Anybody dumb enough to live on a hill in snow country deserves to do the following:

Reward the guy with points for finishing and buy him a beer—yes, even in SLC.

Buy him a set of chains (but not out of the Nut treasury.)

Quit whining." – "Badwater" Bob Spiwak (#2310).

"Finish the round. Getting up the hill is not the issue. I played last week in 30 mph winds with some snow on the ground, and right at 32 degrees. It was supposed to get to 38 to 40, but never made it. A penalty stroke for you, and you buy the beer." - Dan Cedusky (#0470).

"Sounds like #2824 is in for some bonus points. As for you, wait until it snows again; finish the 18 and then, if need be, take a cab home...where are your priorities?" - Mike Brands (#0774).

"You are our leader.....but I do believe that fellow golf nut # 2824 was only following your rules...believing in the spirit of golf that all things can be accomplished on a golf course....I have only quit once during a round, and to this day, I still regret it.....anybody can quit, but the ones who finish play the round as its founders intended it to be played...unless there is a chance of bodily harm, i.e., lightning, etc." - Dave "Iron Byron" Wells (#2705).

"Definitely award the points.... think about his achievement not his 'insubordination' to a higher authority. We must always question and challenge authority... it is what has made this country so great. By the way, did you make it up the hill?" - Gregg "The Dalai Lama" Guernsey (#0006).

"It's NOT #2824's problem that your sprawling mansion sits high on a hill. It's NOT #2824's problem that your driving skills may be suspect. It's NOT #2824's problem that you wimped (yes, WIMPED) out in the face of a gentle breeze and a few flakes. No partial credit for the round. He gets

MEGA-BONUS POINTS....and you get the public humiliation that you deserve. #0001 bails out??? I'm terribly disappointed. Frankly, I'm going to have to rethink this whole GNS thing in light of this story. Wonder if #0002 is ready, willing and able to 'move up' (or down as it were) a number?" - Bob "Captain Hook" Scavetta (#1696).

"If you couldn't have gotten your car up the hill and had to walk,......so? You've done it before would be my guess.....If one Nut could finish, a late-blooming, new Nut to boot, how could you not, being the #1 Nut and all!!! You know, leading by example, etc. Your leaving was kinda like a captain abandoning his ship sorta. I'm think'n maybe you were not doing so well in your match." - Jim Gallagher (#2860).

"Insubordination not! Give #2824 the points. Dereliction of duties, yes! Obviously the course had not become unplayable, since the other three continued. You should have completed the round, and then dealt with the problem of getting home, if there was one. Are you in danger of regaining your sanity? You're a Golf Nut, or you were. Now there's doubt. While playing golf, or even just thinking about playing golf, all other concerns and issues are secondary. P.S. I still can't figure out why you moved from Arizona. What were you thinking?" - Chuck Muehling (#1988).

"You would have been justified only by paying off the Nassau upon walking off the 11th green, with the assumption that you would have lost holes 12-18. Accordingly, you should fine and suspend yourself." - James Dowling (eNut).

"No brainer. Nut points. But you, our fearless leader should have been there at the end. I mean what is another missed dinner?" - Peter Shaerf (#2872).

"If you can't finish what you start, how can you be #0001?" - Peter Moore (#0002).

Tough crowd. The Nuts weighed in, and I got a good tongue-lashing. So the next time it snows, it looks like I'll be finishing the round.

Here are a few more guys who would agree that bad weather is no excuse for not playing:

Don Rose (#0003) - While playing golf in winds gusting to 65 mph, he hit a full driver a total of 24 yards into the teeth of the wind. 124 points.

Marshall Gleason (#0008) - Has participated in seven British Amateurs, never once reaching match play. In his last attempt the 70 mph wind blew off his stocking cap!

Paul Linnman (#0500) - Played golf in a snowstorm on Christmas Day with a local TV weatherman, who promised him good weather. 250 points.

Charles Gilmore (#0861) - Wears padded ski gloves when the temperature drops below freezing. 100 points.

Bill Johnson (#0904) - Has played golf in "Typhoon Condition 1", with wind gusts in excess of 85 mph. Hit a 5-Iron that went all of 42 yards into the wind. 385 points.

Bill Johnson (#0904) - Played golf in Wainright, Alaska in the winter in 25-below temperatures, and on ground that was frozen solid. Putted from 162 yards on the second hole and lipped it out. 162 points.

James Landowski (#1654) - Played for 10 years in the Winterfest golf tournament in Milwaukee. Held in February, the worst weather was 25 below and 1 1/2 feet of snow on the ground. They used yellow tennis balls, rather than golf balls, so they could find the ball. 250 points.

Chuck Muehling (#1998) - Had to ask ice skaters to move aside one December day in Maryland, so he could play to a Par 3 over a frozen pond. 100 points.

Paul Kipp (#2197) - Plays annually in the Groundhog Open in early February in Sterling Heights, Michigan. They pay "white fees" instead of green fees. 200 points.

Michael Petru (#0490) - Is designing a lightweight chest and shoulder harness to hold his golf umbrella in the rain, keeping the hands free for play at all times. 200 points.

"The pro told me these would help."

12th Hole

"I'LL TAKE IT!"

When it comes to spending frenzies, nobody can match golfers. Just tell us the latest driver, putter, or swing gadget is "The Secret," and we'll own it in short order. In my case, you could say I have a "black belt" in shopping when it comes to golf purchases. I can't begin to tell you how many golf clubs I've purchased in my 34 years in the game, but if I ever do count them up, I'm not telling you. You might tell my wife.

A recent example involved "The Prez" (#0003) and Scott Masingill (#0047). I've always played forged blades. I'm not loyal to any one brand; I just went with whichever blade caught my fancy in any given year. I've had Titleist, Wilson, Hogan, MacGregor. You name it, I've had it. A couple of years ago, while playing Mizunos, I decided that I was giving up too much distance with my forged blades. It was a very stressful and traumatic time for me because I had never played cast clubs before. Well, to be honest, there was the time 20 or so years ago when I bought the Ping Eye 2s because they were all the rage, and they nearly ruined me.

Anyway, I'd been thinking about making the move to cast clubs for several months, but hadn't acted on the urge yet. I had a golf trip to Oregon scheduled, to play in the U.S. Amateur qualifier at Waverly Country Club. It was scheduled for a Monday, but I was coming in on Friday to play a practice round with Scott, and then 36 holes a day on Saturday and

Sunday with The Prez and Scott at Eugene Country Club. Not coincidentally, Fiddler's Green—one of the greatest golf superstores on the
planet—also happens to be located in Eugene.

After my less than stellar performance in the Friday practice round, I
decided that the time had come for me to make the switch to cast, so on
the drive to Eugene I hatched the perfect plan. Fiddler's will take trade-ins
on certain brands of clubs—Mizuno being one of them—so I decided to
trade them in on something the next morning. I just didn't know what it
was going to be. There were still a few details to be worked out, such as
the 36 holes we had planned for the next morning, but that was only a
minor problem. Luckily, Fiddler's opens seven days a week at 8 a.m. and
we were there when they took the padlock off the front door. I tried six
different sets of irons, but one set stood out above all the rest: the Taylor
Made Firesole irons with a regular graphite shaft. A regular graphite
shaft!!! Had I gone completely nuts?? Here I was, a forged blade, True
Temper-S300-stiff-steel-shaft kind of guy, going to a regular graphite
shaft just two days before the U.S. Amateur qualifier. Yes, I had gone completely nuts, but I liked them.

Besides, I already had the Firesole driver and 3-wood with a regular,
graphite bubble shaft. Now everything matched. But then there was the
small matter of the 2-iron. Taylor Made didn't make a 2-iron in my new
irons, so I bought a 5-wood to match my driver and 3-wood (a 5-wood!
With a regular graphite shaft! I had lost my mind!). The only thing left
was to get a new putter, so I did that, too. A Wilson 8802 for a hundred
bucks. What the hell, might as well shoot a million in the Amateur qualifier.

Off we sped with my new sticks for 36 a day over two glorious days at
one of the greatest golf courses in the world - Eugene Country Club. And
it was glorious. I hit the ball so well that Scott said, "Head Nut, if you ever
sell those clubs, I'll kick your butt."

A few months later, I traded them in for a set of Firesole Tour models with True Temper S300 steel shafts. So what did you expect me to do? I hated my 5-wood. Every time I looked down at it, it made me feel old. I needed a 2-iron to feel "whole" again, so the graphite-shafted Firesoles had to go.

"Garland changes equipment more than I change underwear," Masingill says. "In Idaho that is once a week. He also changes his swing every day and looks the same as it did in 1980. Perfect."

"Ron buys his equipment with his pro shop credit winnings," adds Judy. "At least that's what he's been telling me all these years. All his clubs are in the attic. I'd love to have a yard sale some day."

Uh, I don't think so.

Anyway, feeling young again, I traded in my Taylor Made Firesole driver for a Titleist 975D driver with a lightweight graphite shaft (Titleist "Green" label). I swapped my Firesole 3-wood for a Titleist 975F fairway wood because I wanted matching woods (I'm sure you understand why this had to be done). But about a week after I bought the new 975D, I was hitting balls at the range with a friend of mine who had the same driver but with the new EI-70 shaft. I hit it a couple of times and drove over to Uinta Golf in Salt Lake City and traded my new 975 for one with the EI-70 shaft.

A few months later, I "quit the game forever" again, and didn't play golf for six months. I sold my new irons and woods back to Uinta Golf for merchandise credit in their store. When I made my comeback several months later, I didn't have any new clubs, so I went into the attic and pulled out my old 1978 MacGregor Muirfield irons, some of my old persimmon woods, and my old "Wilson designed by Arnold Palmer" putter.

I played with them for the rest of the year, and had a wonderful time remembering just how damned hard this game used to be before high-tech nuclear rocket launchers and plastic explosives replaced real clubs and real balls.

One of my all-time favorite "club nuts" is Nut #2022, Jerry Lacey. Jerry is constantly buying new equipment, and spending a lot of money on it, too. And he always has them sent "Overnight Priority Delivery."

He was in bed, channel surfing at 2:00 a.m. late one night when he came across an infomercial for the "FiberSpeed 2000" driver. He sat there and watched the entire half-hour commercial while sitting in bed, then picked up the phone, dialed the number, and ordered one. When he told me about the purchase a few days later, he said, "Can you believe it? The first time I dialed the number, the line was busy. At 2 o'clock in the morning!"

Two weeks later, he heard about the exciting, new $1,700 Maruman "Suppan Tap" driver, and ordered one of those. Three weeks later, a friend told him about the "Zircon 1" driver and, of course, he ordered one the same day—Overnight Delivery.

Jerry doesn't limit his impulses to just drivers either. A few years back, he heard about the hot new "Snake Eyes" sand wedges, and ordered two— a 56- and a 60-degree. While he was on the phone to Edwin Watts Mail-order Golf Company he decided it was time to buy a new set of irons, and added a set of the ultraexpensive, Mizuno MP29 irons with the special nickel alloy to his shopping list. The sand wedges were $200 each, and the MP29s another $1,200. Now that's the kind of shopping that'll earn you a "black belt." Oh, and just in case the specs are off when his new clubs arrive, he has his own lie and loft machine at home, too.

And if you don't think golf nuts know equipment, here's one for you. Van Robinson – Nut #1615 – and I were sitting on the 18th tee of the Phoenix Open a few years back, watching the players come through. Knowing that he was a real equipment nut, I started asking him what each of them had in their bags. He told me what woods they were playing, their irons, the brand and lofts of the sand wedges, and the type of ball they used. He could even tell me if they had a mixed bag of irons.

We did about five or six groups, and he nailed every player. We weren't close enough to the players for him to actually see their equipment, so he was reeling this stuff off from memory. Now that's commitment. I was impressed. I gave him a ton of Nut points.

This equipment thing works the other way around, too. "I was wearing knickers before the late Payne Stewart," says Joe Malay, the first Golf Nut of the Year. "I had a 56-inch driver before Rocky Thompson. And I had four wedges in my bag before any of the Tour players did. Guys like Ron Garland and Don Rose can afford to buy their equipment. I have to create mine. I build clubs around my game. They build their game around their clubs. I once had a club I called a '369.' It had the shaft of a 3-iron, the loft of a 6-iron and the head of a 9-iron. I could hit it about 225 yards."

Joe Malay aside, here are a few other Nuts who've earned their "black belt" at the local pro shop:

Ken Huckins (#0409) - Spent more than $3,000 on golf equipment in his first two months as a golfer, not including green fees, range balls, instruction books or lessons. 300 points.

Ronn Grove (#0830) - At one time he had 54 putters, 22 pairs of golf slacks, 35 golf shirts, six sets of irons, 12 drivers, five wedges and five tour staff golf bags. In 1983 he used all 54 putters. 554 points.

Don Rose (#0003) - He placed 48 of his used putters on consignment in the pro shop at his home club for 90 days. None sold. 480 points.

Marshall Gleason (#0008) - Paid more than $1,000 for a set of Tommy Armour 645s irons when he feared that his Pings were about to be ruled illegal due to the groove controversy. He never used them, as the lawsuit was settled within a month of his purchase. He then purchased a backup set of the previously illegal Ping irons. 200 points.

J.W. Baker III (#0230) - Purchased two sets of Ping irons, 1 set of Axiom irons, eight different combinations of metal woods, two Power Pod drivers and four different putters in the span of 120 days. 314 points.

Ken Huckins (#0409) - Lost 25 golf balls in 18 holes of golf. Returned to the pro shop three times to buy more ammo, finally finishing in total darkness with a ball from a playing companion. 250 points.

George Mack Sr. (#0460) – At one time he had 24 color-coordinated outfits, including shoes. 240 points.

Tex Hollenberger (#0976) - Has 13 full sets of clubs, and has a name for each club in his bag. His preshot routine includes talking to his club, addressing the club by its name and telling it what he wants it to do. 214 points.

Burt Hotchkiss (#1165) - Built a nine-hole course on his farm. 1,900 points.

John Rodgers (#2311) - Attended the Ralph Maltby Golf Club Repair School in Newark, Ohio. He arrived with 40 pounds of golf components and left with 165 pounds of clubs, equipment, and components. 500 points.

Johnny Curtis (#0573) - Once bought a Cobalt/Chromium HM-50 graphite-shafted driver from fellow golf nut Jim Nielsen (#0859) for $175. He then sold it back to him two months later for $50. Shrewd. 225 points.

13th Hole

THE COLLECTORS

I am proud to say that I'm not one of those "collector" types. I mean, what kind of guy would collect golf balls, for crying out loud? Or bag tags? Or divot repair tools? Or ball markers? Or logo caps? Or golf pencils, for goodness sakes! Or. . . . well, you get the idea. There's got to be something wrong with these people, don't you think? It's sick. I mean, really sick. I think they must be a little nuts.

Of course, the fact that I have every single issue of *Golf Digest* and *Golf Magazine* since 1969—the year I started playing golf—stashed away in boxes in my attic doesn't make me a collector, does it? At least the magazines have some utilitarian value. At one time they were actually read before they were tucked safely into the attic (now there's a scary thought—I read every page of every single one of those magazines that are now in my attic. Hmmmm.).

My wife still hasn't forgiven me for collecting—I mean keeping—them. They've stayed with us through seven moves in thirty years of marriage, and I hear about the magazines every time we move. I must say—in only a small concession to her point—that a box full of magazines is really heavy. But I only have 20 or 30 boxes of the things now. Kind of a sore subject with Mrs. Nut.

Anyway, back to my point. I don't think I should be considered a "collector" just because I save past issues of golf magazines. I also don't think that keeping scorecards for every round that I played for a period of several years should be held against me either. After all, I didn't just write down my score. I charted my rounds on those scorecards. I kept track of fairways hit; greens in regulation; distance from hole on approach shots; putts; birdies, OBs, lost balls, water balls, and the number of "good shots" hit on each hole. Those scorecards are filled with valuable data. Not to mention the wonderful memories of all those "others" I've made on golf holes over the years.

And we certainly can't count all of the old clubs in the attic. Why, the only reason I still have them is that nobody would want them. They're old. Some of them are even made out of persimmon (whatever that is).

And then there are the trophies (my favorite is the one for winning low net in the 13th flight of my member-guest one year). I'd throw them in the garbage except that I'm afraid the garbage man would think I was just bragging again.

Oh, and did I mention that I have film of my swing dating back to the early 1970s? Actually, I have every foot of film I have ever taken of my swing since the early 1970s. It probably adds up to over a mile of tape and film, but I'm a little afraid to measure it. I'm up to several boxes now, all labeled and dated, starting with the 8mm film I mentioned earlier, and I'm still going. But I'm only keeping those tapes and reels because I may need to refer back to them someday, even if only to see what kind of clothes I wore back then.

Anyway, I just wanted to make it crystal clear I am not a "collector." At least not in the classic sense. Now that we've cleared that up, let's talk about some real collectors. These Nuts are really "nuts!"

I've already talked about 1995 Golf Nut of the Year Mike Noyes's "collection addiction," so I won't go into that again, except to say that his book collection probably increased 20 per cent during the time that it took me to type this sentence.

"At first when I decided to collect golf stuff I got everything, so I have subcollections of clubs, balls, tees, pottery, games, etc," Noyes says. "Somewhere I realized I was running out of room, had too much crap, and my wife was getting ticked off.

"I solved the latter problem by buying something for her collection (Depression Era glass) every time I got something. But she's on to me and wants no more. In any case I have friends in the book business and love their shops. Between them and thrift stores it's just been building up but at a much slower pace nowadays."

One time I found a book about the Champions Golf Course with the inscription "To Jackie Pung, always a champion in my book" and thought it strange it should be in circulation. I wrote Jackie and found it had been stolen so I sent it back to her. Now I am her angel.

When you talk about collectors, there are those who "collect golf stuff" (I guess I'd have to admit I'm in that category, but don't tell Mrs. Nut. On second thought, she already knows) and then there are "world-class collectors." Unlike me, they usually carve out an area of specialty such as ball markers or golf pencils or scorecards.

One of those world-class types is a proud member of our small band of rebels. His name is Greg Miles, Nut #2681,and he makes guys like Mike Noyes sit up and take notice. But what makes Greg so interesting is that he's a multidiscipline collector. He collects logo golf balls and golf caps. And boy does he ever! Well, here, let him tell you:

Miles: "While my collection also includes sport teams, colleges, etc. (which would increase my total number) my current golf-related logo ball collection presently stands at 10,617."

He then goes on to break them down by category: Different Course Logos: 6,056, Duplicate Course Logos: 997, Golf Tournament Logos: 1,471. Greg's logo cap collection, while not nearly as plentiful, is every bit as impressive. At last reckoning he had 113 logo golf caps, which he describes as: "embroidered golf logo baseball-style caps, not including visors, fedoras, Hogan-style caps, or knit ski caps."

What makes this so interesting is that he stores them in a (very large) closet on several custom-built shelves. He even has gone so far as to catalog his caps by type of logo, type of fabric (nylon, cotton, twill, corduroy), and color. He recently moved to a new, larger home so he would have enough room to store/display his balls and caps. No surprise there.

"Of the current *Golf Digest* America's Top 100," Miles boasts, "I have 94 and need six. But as that list changes every two years, it becomes an ongoing quest."

Just about every "golf nut" collects golf balls. We find a brand new Titleist in the rough, and our heart races. We put it in our bag, and save it for a special occasion. Or we find a ball with a ding or two and it goes into our shag bag. Rarely does a golfer find a golf ball on the golf course and just leave it there. We pick it up, put it in our golf bag, and put it to some good use at a later date. Like using it as a "water ball" on that damned par 3 with the 200-yard carry over the lake on the back nine.

Kathy Beallo takes ball collecting to another level. Here is a woman who uses a round of golf as just another excuse to collect golf balls. She doesn't keep them, mind you. She just likes to find them. Then she gives them to her friends, who play golf with them. It's a public service kind of thing with her. Or perhaps it's just an obsession.

It got so bad that she bought a "golf ball rake" that she saw in a golf catalog. It's a contraption that looks like a garden rake, except it doesn't have a handle. Instead, it has a long rope attached to it, and you toss it out into a lake and drag it back in. It bounces along the bottom of the lake, and when you've hauled it back to shore there are golf balls lodged between its tongs.

So if you're ever playing Spyglass Hill along Monterey's 17-Mile Drive and you spot a perky lady dragging one of the lakes, just holler out, "Hi Kathy!" It will be her. She and her husband have a home that borders one of its fairways.

Like I said, she doesn't need the golf balls.

And then there's the story of "lucky" Tom Jewell, Nut #0175 and 1997 Golf Nut of the Year. Tom's prize possession is an autographed 8 x 10 photo taken of him and Ben Hogan at the Waldorf Astoria in New York in 1988. One day a repairman came to do some work at Tom's home, and as it turned out, he was a golfer. Tom took the photo off his wall, brought it into the garage and showed it to him, then laid it on the trunk of his car while he wrote the repairman a check for the work.

Unfortunately, Tom forgot about the photo, leaving it on the trunk. A little while later his wife drove to the grocery store, and after about two miles, while stopped at a light, she heard a knock on the window. She opened the window to find a complete stranger standing there, holding the photo, which was in perfect condition. It had stayed on the trunk the entire way. If he had lost or damaged the photo, it would most certainly have been irreplaceable because he didn't have a negative of the photo.

Don't try to tell Tom that the "golf gods" weren't looking out for him that day. However, if he had lost the photo he wouldn't have wanted for a "crying towel." He is the proud owner of 72 logo golf towels – a GNS record.

And as long as we're talking about golf towels, I must mention Mike Brands. His total is 46 logo towels, but he goes 1-up on Jewell because all of his are displayed. He uses them as hand towels in his home or in his cottage on the Oregon coast. At home, he has a room that has been dubbed "Golfland" because all the walls and flat surfaces are covered with golf paraphernalia that he has collected over the years. And that's where you'll find some of the towels, along with a lot of other "stuff," as my wife likes to call it.

"You gotta love golf," says Mike.

Here are a few other "Collector Nuts" who don't quite measure up to #2681's prodigious performance, but they're still "nuts" nonetheless:

Jeffrey August (#1707) - Has over 11,000 bag tags from around the world, and carries 15 on his bag at all times. 1,115 points.

Howdy Giles (#2073) - Arnold Palmer's personal dentist, he has a gold ball marker made from the gold in Arnie's fillings. 2,000 points.

Don Scott (#1708) - Has more than 23,000 scorecards. 2,300 points.

Jeff Lines (#0118) - Videotapes and saves the telecasts of every round of golf's majors each year. 400 points.

Jane Minesinger (#1978) - Has 796 divot repair tools. 1,796 points.

Daniel Cedusky (#0470) - Cuts out all of the "good" golf tips from golf magazines, and files them according to subject in indexed three-ring binders. 300 points.

Charles Gilmore (#0861) - Owns more than 2,000 golf balls, most of which he keeps in an old freezer. 200 points.

Leo Kelly (#1689) - Has commandeered more than one-fifth of the floor space in his home in order to display his antique golf club collection. He also followed the PGA Tour for three years, displaying his antique golf club collection. 1,503 points.

Nobby Orens (#2259) - Has 292 logo golf shirts. ("I don't remember exactly why I started a 'collection,'" Orens says. "But when I started playing golf I really didn't have any 'golf' shirts so I started buying them as a memento of each golf course I played, along with a logo ball.") 1,292 points.

Howie Smith (#0283) - Has 49 logo golf sweaters (he lives in the Pacific Northwest, so he needs them). 1,049 points.

Boyd Sempel (#1085) - Is the proud owner of 24,000 ball markers (which is probably a world record, but who's counting?) 2,400 points.

Sempel and Minesinger, by the way, are in contact with each other.

"Boyd Sempel, the main ball marker man, has sent me a number of new ones recently," Minesinger reports. "None are displayed since I have 2,100 logo balls on display as well as four-glass enclosed cases of ball markers. Most plastic and some metal tools are mounted on foam board — the balance stored in boxes — and, yes, I do go through them on a regular basis for my own amusement and amazement.

"I am not a good enough golfer to hit the shot that hits, bites, and makes a mark, but I have fixed so many marks that I had to retire one metal tool—it was almost knife sharp. With arthritic hands, I prefer the tool with the money clip back or round ball indent on the back. Never collected anything 'til I took up golf and now ....! I am not as nuts as some, but my friends think I am the nuttiest one they know."

14th Hole

THE TRULY COMMITTED

As our motto states, "You've Got To Be Committed!" At least that's the way we feel about it. If you haven't figured it out already, we reward Nuts with big bonus points for showing true "commitment." And we *really* reward behavior that would get them committed.

As I've mentioned earlier, it all started when I did some pretty bizarre things that made my friends just shake their heads in amazement and say things like, "Garland, you've got to be nuts!"

Heck, they didn't seem bizarre to me

I was just trying to discover "The Secret."

I knew it was out there, and if I could just discover it, I would never ever, ever, ever hit a bad shot again. At least that's what I thought. I know it sounds irrational, but every Golf Nut worth his salt feels exactly the same way. Why do you think we do the strange things that we do? Do you think we get up in the morning and say, "Gee, I wonder how I can make a fool of myself in front of my family and friends today?" No, it's much more subtle than that. It's probably more like drug addiction. We've just got to have our "fix" for the day, and there's not much we won't do to get it. Oh, and just for the record, 34 years later, I'm still searching for the freakin' Secret.

One of my favorite antics didn't involve any prior planning or, for that matter, much conscious thought either. I always keep my clubs in the trunk of my car because you never know when opportunity will strike and I might have time to hit a quick bucket or roll a few putts. And I almost always played golf after work in those days, so I needed the sticks with me at all times. One day I was on my way to work when I spotted flames coming out the rear of my car as I drove down the freeway. Needless to say, I was afraid that the car might blow up, so I quickly pulled over and ran for cover. Oh, did I mention that before I ran for cover, I opened the trunk and grabbed my clubs? I mean, what is life when compared to life without golf?

What was I supposed to do, let them go up in flames? I will admit that I was half scared to death during those few seconds when I was opening the trunk and pulling the clubs out. I had visions of the gas tank exploding and ending my golf career, not to mention my life, but I had to get those clubs. My briefcase? I left it in the car.

As long as we're talking about commitment, there was the time that I thought Mrs. Nut was definitely going to have me committed. The Oregon Amateur was being held in Medford and we were living upstate in Portland, some five hours away. The state Open started the Monday after the state Amateur, and it was another three hours back upstate to Sunriver Resort in Bend. I took a couple of weeks of vacation, and drove to Medford for the Amateur. It was a week-long match play event that started on Monday with a two-day 36-hole medal play qualifying round. My plan was to drive the five hours to Medford, last as long as possible in the tournament, then drive five hours home, play a little golf for the rest of whatever was left of the week, and then drive with the family to Sunriver for the Oregon Open.

Things went better than expected, and I made it all the way to the finals. That was the good news. The bad news was that the finals were on Sunday, and I needed to be in Sunriver with my family on Monday. But they were still in Portland. How could I finish a 36-hole match in Medford, drive five hours to Portland, pick them up, and then drive 3 1/2 hours to Bend all in one day? The answer is that I couldn't. So on Saturday evening, when the full gravity of the situation struck me, I called Mrs. Nut and suggested that she and the kids catch an early morning flight to Medford, rent a car, and get to the golf course as soon as they could. The alternative was to cancel out of the Oregon Open, but that didn't even cross my mind. What kind of vacation would it be if I'm in Sunriver and not playing in the Oregon Open?

To make a long story short, the Nut Family made it to Medford, and we all had the great pleasure of watching Tony Joyner birdie the first five holes of the afternoon round and thump me 4 & 3. Then we returned the rental car and piled into the family car for the three hour drive to Sunriver, arriving late that evening. Then I got up early the next morning for the first round of the Oregon Open.

Oh, did I mention the other two tournaments that followed the Oregon Open? Small detail. We drove another four hours to Coos Bay for the Southwest Oregon Amateur, and then back to Bend for the Mirror Pond Amateur. The stats on that little two-week adventure added up to 1,480 miles and 293 holes of tournament golf; 121 of which were played in 107-degree temperatures at 36 holes a day. (You've got to be committed.)

Hey, I'm not the only one who's nuts around here. Listen to this story about The Duke of the Desert. Duke DeBernardi (#0889) is not just a golf nut, he's a Masters nut, too. He lives for that tournament every year, and doesn't miss a single minute of the daily telecasts. But like many of us, he had never attended the tournament in person. He decided one year that he was going, no matter what. Period. End of story. He was going to the Masters.

One small problem: he didn't have a ticket. However, when he was in college he had played on the same Oregon Duck golf team as Peter Jacobsen, and "Jake" had qualified for that year's event. Actually, Jacobsen getting his invitation to the Masters was a story in itself. I'll let Duke tell it:

"I went to watch 'Peter Jake' (Jacobsen) play on Saturday in Phoenix that year and found him on the practice green with caddie Fluff Cowan. He had missed the cut by one shot and Fluff said he missed every shot he looked at. I watched him putt and he was stroking it better than ever and explaining that he had been working with Dave Pelz on his short game. He asked me what I thought and I told him it looked great and watched him stripe it on the range for about an hour before I told him I knew he was going to win because he was swinging and stroking it so well.

"I told him to do it [win] before the Masters because I had never gone and really wanted to go. My friends razzed me about Jake missing the cut here [Phoenix] since I told them he was hitting it great and had sent notes to my mother and sister to watch for him to win soon. So when he won the next two tournaments at Pebble Beach and San Diego, I looked like a golf guru and called Peter's brother, David, to see about going to Augusta.

"The trip was a little hairy because the tickets weren't for sure and I could only go for the weekend due to business. So I got on a flight via Minneapolis Friday morning and missed connections to Atlanta. I took a cab to the Mall of America near MSP airport and watched some of the Masters in a bar with no sound before going back to the airport and getting a red-eye out, arriving in Atlanta early Saturday morning.

"I then rented a car and drove to Augusta as fast as possible. I got there and hooked up with 'David Jake' (Peter's brother), got my ticket and hoofed it over to the practice tee to watch the greatest golfers in the world up close. I followed Peter the full 18 that day and Sunday. I also followed the leaders. He was in contention until he hit it into Rae's Creek in front of 13 on Sunday.

"Another Oregon golfer, Brian Henninger was in the last group on Sunday with Crenshaw and we caught up with him and his dad, Wayne, at TBones Sunday night to talk about the Masters. It was the most fun I ever had watching a tournament. It was like visiting a shrine that I had worshipped since childhood. I will treasure the memory forever."

Dan Cedusky (#0470) is crazy in a vagabond kind of way. He has been to several psychiatrists and hypnotists in an attempt to quit the game. It hasn't helped him quit, but it has helped him reduce his handicap by three strokes. 300 points. He once played 18 holes so early one morning that he was leaving the parking lot as the pro was arriving to open the course. 180 points.

"Boy that's been a while ago," Cedusky says. "I have just started playing again after a layoff of three years. . . divorce. . . moving around, clubs stolen several times . . . long story. The Golf Nuts Society tracked me down and got me playing again with a few 2002 Christmas presents of clubs, balls, and bag. My last full year of golf was 1992. With so many Nuts sending words of support I had to start again.

"Beating the pro to the course happened to me several times when I was traveling. I got so busy, I couldn't get out. So occasionally I would find a course between my motel and work site I was visiting. I would get up early, go to the course, carry a few clubs in my hand or bag and walk as many holes as I could before a quick change and off to work.

"Several times I finished nine holes before 7 a.m. in colder weather when no one was out. I'd stop at the pro shop while he was making coffee, have a cup and pay. Usually he wouldn't charge me. Then I would go to work. I can't, for the life of me, remember the courses. One was way out southwest of Chicago near a Holiday Inn. Another one was near Paris, IL and one near Marion, IL. I played five holes just as sunup was coming twice at Fort Leavenworth, KS in about October of 1985.

"I was having some marital problems due to depression, work stress, and too much golf. I saw a shrink several times. It didn't save my marriage but helped my attitude enough and lowered my handicap by three strokes. It's kind of foggy now. That was 10 to 12 years ago. If the shrink hadn't charged so much, I would have gone to him more and also would have had him talk to my wife. Maybe it would have saved my marriage and lowered my scores even more. But I couldn't afford him."

Here are a some more Nuts who should be committed:

Jeff Leinassar (#0009) - A dentist, he has a putting cup embedded in the floor of the waiting room, complete with putters and balls, so his patients can putt while they wait. 300 points.

Marty Price (#0038) - After developing tendinitis in his wrist, he switched to playing left-handed to relieve the pain, refusing to heed his doctor's advice to stop playing for a few months. 650 points.

Scott Masingill (#0047) - When informed he needed corrective surgery on his wrists, he flew to Los Angeles and had famed orthopedic surgeon Dr. Robert Kerlan design and rebuild them specifically for golf. 1,000 points.

Norman Brenner (#0065) - Played golf three days after a vasectomy. 300 points.

Bob Ball (#0069) - Is the first man to achieve the "GNS Slam," playing golf on New Year's Day, Easter, Mother's Day, Thanksgiving and Christmas in a single year. 1,000 points.

Chris Veitch (#0151) - Drove the 435 miles from Orange County, CA to Monterey and back in a single day to play a practice round for the California Amateur. He left at 4:00 a.m. to make his noon tee time, played the course in two hours in a cart, and was home by 10:00 p.m. 870 points.

Stan Buratto (#0222) - Played a round of golf while on crutches, and on another occasion, with his arm in a cast. 1,000 points.

Walt Chambers (#0286) - Organized and played in the Fur Rendezvous Golf Tournament in Anchorage, Alaska. Shovels, brooms, and ice picks were allowed but counted toward the 14-club maximum. 200 points.

John Day (#0402) - Drove his motor home 1,200 miles across America with his golf clubs stored in the toilet due to lack of storage space. Sadly, he was only able to use them twice on the entire trip. 120 points.

Bob McCormick (#0404) - Built a nine-hole golf course by himself on his cattle ranch in Atoka, OK, and began teaching the local ranchers how to play so he would have playing companions. 900 points.

George Mack Sr. (#0460) - Flew to Scottsdale twice in the same month to take a lesson from famous golf instructor Jim Flick. The second lesson was taken in a hailstorm. 200 points.

Jeff Larsen (#0467) - Played in the first annual Golf Nuts Society tournament with his right arm in a cast. 1,000 points.

Bob Miller (#0677) - Played 600 holes of miniature golf in 24 hours in a local fundraiser. 600 points.

Virginia Bushnell (#0553) - At age 59 she played 100 holes of golf in a single day, walking and carrying her clubs. 1,059 points.

Steve Post (#0623) - Convinced his hunting partners to move their annual October hunting camp next to the six-hole Fossil Kinzu Golf Course, which is out in the middle of nowhere. 106 points.

Dwane Brands (#0786) - In 1932, he climbed Mt. Hood with a 5-iron strapped to his back. Upon reaching the summit, he sent a ball sailing down the north slope. 505 points.

Mike Brands (#0774) - Was arrested by an Arizona park ranger and threatened with attempted manslaughter for hitting golf shots off the south rim of the Grand Canyon. He plea-bargained, pleading guilty to the reduced charge of littering, and paid the $15 fine. Like father, like son. 515 points.

Phil Spiesman (#0825) - Had a knee operation, and was told by his doctor to leave the cast on for six weeks. Was also told not to play golf during the recovery period. One week later, he cut off the cast with a power saw and teed it up. 206 points.

Bill Johnson (#0904) - Has hit balls into the Atlantic and Pacific Oceans, the China Sea, and the Gulf of Mexico. 140 points.

Jack Rickard (#1033) - In Salt Lake City for a convention, he had been promised left- handed clubs and a pair of golf shoes by the golf staff, but upon arrival at the course neither were available. Undeterred, he teed off barefoot, with left-handed woods and right-handed irons. 300 points.

J. Michael McGowan (#1054) - Has played golf for 33 years despite being allergic to grass, having a bad back, and having survived a skin cancer operation. Has been advised against playing golf by his doctor, chiropractor, and physical therapist. He has ignored them all. 333 points.

Rob Croskrey (#1060) - Played in a full leg cast for six months. 600 points.

Lawton Harrison (#1093) - Occasionally plays cross-country golf naked at night so he can "be one with nature and play totally by feel." 1,000 points.

More Lawton Harrison (#1093) - Once played home from the local tavern at midnight, with a 1-iron and a whiffle ball. The distance was five miles, and "the sparks were flyin'!" reports Lawton. 1,000 points.

Lawton Harrison (yet again) (#1093) - Watched the lunar eclipse on August 17, 1989 and then went out and played a few holes in the dark to celebrate. 200 points.

Scott Houston (#1186) - Has played Cypress Point, Pebble Beach, Poppy Hills, Spanish Bay, and Spyglass Hill at night. 500 points.

Scott Houston (again) (#1186) - Once hit a golf shot in every state in New England (New York, Connecticut, Massachusetts, Vermont, New Hampshire, Maine and Rhode Island) in a single day. 700 points.

Walt McGinnis (#1907) - Went to the car dealer to have his car serviced. While he was there he filled out a sweepstakes entry for an all-expense paid trip to the U.S. Open and won. 500 points.

John Yznaga (#1935) - Suffers from tennis elbow on both elbows, but refuses to allow it to keep him off the course. He plays every day, and his premedication routine includes six Advil, two elbow straps with built-in heating pads, and a wrist strap with a built-in liquid mercury shock absorber. His postround medication consists of an 18-ounce Jose Cuervo Tequila Popper and ice packs on both elbows. 575 points.

Al Schleunes (#1965) - Taped the U.S. Senior Open and the Western Open on two separate VCRs on the same day, since they were telecast at the same time on different networks and he was playing golf during both telecasts. 200 points.

Bob Van Nest (#1975) - Has played golf in 54 countries, a Golf Nuts Society record. 540 points.

Ed Gowan (#1982) - Drove from Cleveland to Tampa on a Friday for a weekend of golf. Was back in Cleveland by Monday afternoon. 1,000 points.

Earl Kulson (#2005) - Played golf in 122 degree heat in Phoenix. The airport was closed because it was too hot for jets to fly. 122 points.

Nick Nikrant (#2021) - Named his son Jack Nicklaus Nikrant after his idol, Jack Nicklaus. His in-laws would not speak to him for months because of his decision. 300 points.

David Hales (#2156) - Slipped and fell on the second tee during a recent round, breaking his right leg in the fall. Unaware that his leg was broken, he finished the round.. "I had been getting too much weight on my right side on the backswing, but couldn't do it after I broke my leg, and I had my best round in years." Convinced he had discovered "The Secret," Hales talked his doctor into fitting him with a special brace that allowed him to play in his club's upcoming member-guest tournament despite the broken leg. 300 points.

Bob Spiwak (#2310) - While stepping off the third tee box during the first round of a tournament, he injured his right foot. As he continued to play, the pain got worse. He completed the round, went to see a doctor, and played the next day in a cast. He later learned from his doctor that he had broken a bone in his foot. 500 points.

"Nice shot, Mr. Palmer!"

15th Hole

"I LOVE THIS GAME!"

One of my favorite golf quotes is, "If women treated me the way golf does, I wouldn't have anything to do with women."

So what's the big deal about golf? Why do we "Golf Nuts" love this game so much, especially considering the way it treats us? I'm not sure that anyone really knows, but I did have an interesting conversation with a psychiatrist once (no, I wasn't a patient—not that I couldn't use the help), and he said something I've never forgotten. He was a golfer himself, and I was describing our little society to him, telling him some of the same stories you've been reading.

After a couple of the stories, I casually mentioned that, in my opinion, golf was more addictive than alcohol or drugs.

"We hit one shot perfectly, and then it could be several shots, or even several rounds, later before we hit another one that well. But we're hooked on that feeling, and we chase it with fanatical zeal."

"Have you ever heard of 'intermittent reinforcement?'" he asked.

"No, I haven't." I replied.

"It's the most effective way to produce addictive behavior, and it is exactly what you just described."

So there you have it; the best explanation that this "golf nut" has ever heard to describe what's wrong with a whole lot of my friends and me.

Now here are three stories that will give you a glimpse into the mind of a "golf nut," and hopefully explain why we're not afraid to say, "I love this game!"

MY FIRST MASTERS:

By T.H. Nut (me)

4/10/97 - I'm pretty pumped today, because tonight at 11:05 p.m. I fly to Atlanta (arriving at 5:30 a.m.) where I rent a car and drive the two hours to Augusta where I will attend my FIRST Masters. Major points. (Pardon the pun, but I couldn't resist.) I'll be there for three days, returning on Monday morning. It should be great, considering it is Tiger Woods's first Masters as a professional, Greg Norman's first Masters since the gag of the century, and Arnie's return from prostate cancer surgery. Long live the King.

I am a little bummed, however, since I won't be able to defend my club championship title. But considering all of the controversy at the club right now, I wasn't very interested in playing anyway.

4/11/97 - I arrived at the Atlanta airport at 5:30 a.m. after my red-eye flight from Phoenix; "shut-eye" was a grand total of two hours. But never mind. This is The Masters. I knew it was going to be a great weekend when I got a green rental car without even asking. It was destiny. The 140-mile drive seemed to take forever, but it was actually only two hours, including a brief stop for breakfast "to go" from Burger King (two egg & cheese croissants and two milks, please; hold the ham). My average speed was about 85 mph, and I kept all four wheels on the road at all times (I think).

As I approached Augusta I was struck by the powerful influence of this man named Bobby Jones. It seemed that everything was named "Jones," including one of the freeways, the Bobby Jones Expressway. And then it appeared: Washington Road. A name etched into the consciousness of every golf nut who ever laced up a pair of spikes. It conjured up images of dogwoods, azaleas, southern mansions draped with wisteria vines, Magnolia Lane and The Masters.

Boy, was I surprised. As I exited the freeway I was slapped in the face by reality. I was in an area just like any other suburb in America. Motels, fast food restaurants and strip malls dotted the landscape on both sides of Washington Road as I turned right and began the 3-mile drive to the Augusta National Golf Club. As I got closer to my destination I spotted a giant 20-foot hedge consisting of a variety of flowering plants and trees that created an impregnable barrier between the outside world and The Magic Kingdom of Golf—Augusta National Golf Club. The hedge seemed to stretch forever as it encircled the grounds of all that is Augusta National.

I parked my car in the shopping center parking lot across the street from the "walk-in" gate on Washington Road ($10 All Day) and walked briskly to the gate since it was approaching 8:30 a.m. and my appointment with destiny. I was to meet Rob Gillette, 1996 Golf Nut of the Year, who would have a Masters Badge for me. The most difficult ticket in all of sports, and I was about to receive a badge for the last three rounds of The Masters. There is nothing left to say.

After finding Rob and picking up my badge, I had a brief meeting with a sports marketing firm in a restaurant directly across Washington Road from Magnolia Lane. After the meeting, I stood on the curbside for a few minutes, gazing across the street and down the most famous private drive in the world. The magnolias were so huge they formed a canopy over the 300-yard-long lane. There was a small, white brick guardhouse on the right side, and an even smaller white brick gatepost on the left, framing the entrance. As I looked down Magnolia Lane I could see portions of the circle drive, the flowers that form the Augusta National logo, and a small section of the famous clubhouse entrance. I couldn't help but imagine how many great golfers had driven down that lane.

After enjoying this magnificent view, and marveling at the incredible contrast between it and the bustle of the city street called Washington Road, I walked the 100 yards to the "walk-in" gate and stepped onto the hallowed grounds of the Augusta National Golf Club. Well, at least I thought I was stepping onto the hallowed grounds of the Augusta

National Golf Club. Yes, I was inside the giant hedge, and the land was the property of Augusta National, but this was not a golf course. It was a huge parking lot. And I mean huge!! It seemed to stretch forever. It even had its own dogleg, and it probably held more than a thousand cars.

After the 200-yard walk across the parking lot I was standing in front of the "Patrons" entrance, which looked like any other entrance to a sporting event. It was a permanent structure with 8-10 gates where attendants took your badge and ran it through a scanner to make sure it wasn't a forgery. Only then were you allowed into the Augusta National Golf Club and The Masters.

As I walked through the gate, I found myself in a paved, park-like area with flowers, park benches, flagpoles with flags from all countries of the world. On my right was a giant, 4,000 square foot permanent structure filled with "patrons" purchasing Masters logo merchandise, and on my left was a small open-air museum and concession stand. As I passed through this area, I had my first glimpse of the golf course. I was about 100-yards to the right of the clubhouse and the first tee.

The first fairway was directly in front of me, with the first green up the hill to my right. Directly to my right was the official scoreboard, the most massive scoreboard I had ever seen. It was approximately 30-40 feet wide and 20-25 feet high. To my left was the first of the "cabins." They were white, "Old South" architecture, and were connected by breezeways; more like upscale resort lodging units. The pro shop was in the middle of this row of beautiful small "cabins," and at the top of the hill they connected with the clubhouse, which was situated under the most massive oak tree I had ever seen.

On the other side of the clubhouse there were more cabins, and in front of these cabins was the famous grass patio area where the "insiders" enjoyed good food and good company. The clubhouse area was less than fifty yards from the first tee, and was at the highest point on the property.

As I gazed out across the most famous piece of golf real estate in the world, I was struck by its openness. Television just doesn't do it justice. Everything seems to begin and end at the "Big Oak" below the clubhouse at the top of the hill. The first tee was just below the tree, with the ninth green just to its left and slightly down the hill.

The 18th green was a few yards further left; the putting green was just above the 18th green. The 10th tee was beneath the putting green, situated alongside a row of huge Georgia pines. Beside the 10th tee and extending back toward the clubhouse were a series of larger "cabins" — the Eisenhower and others — with the famous "Butler" cabin situated at a 45-degree angle between this row of home-size cabins and the clubhouse cabins at the top of the hill. The golf course essentially extends out from this central point, across the huge open meadow-like area and into the trees, giving Augusta National a magnificent blend of holes, some links-like and others parkland. Holes #4, #5, #6, and #7 on the front nine, and Amen Corner (#11, #12, and #13) on the back are very secluded holes that extend along the perimeter of the golf course far from the clubhouse.

Amen Corner is everything I imagined it to be, and more. It is both beautiful and challenging. I would liken it to my favorite stretch of holes in the world, Cypress Point's #15, #16, and #17. Of the three on Amen Corner, the 11th is my favorite. It is a downhill, 455-yard par 4 that requires the golfer to hit a fade out of a chute of trees to a right-to-left sloping fairway. You are then faced with a downhill approach shot over a small lake to a very small green with bunkers framing the back of the green. It is a spectacularly beautiful and equally difficult hole.

I spent the first day hurrying (no running at The Masters) around the golf course like a young boy on his first trip to Disneyland, just trying to drink it all in. I joined Rob Gillette in following Ben Crenshaw for his entire round. Rob is the founder of Ben's Battalion, and I was proud to wear the official cap as we rooted for Ben, the nicest, most genuine man in all of professional golf. He also put on a pretty incredible charge to go from nine over and "out" for the weekend as he stood on the 12th tee, to

4-over par standing on the 16th tee and a definite for weekend duty. He birdied the 12th from 12 feet, eagled the 13th from 15 feet, and eagled 15 from 22 feet. After Crenshaw's round, I hurried over to the back nine to watch Tiger Woods finish his round. Nothing spectacular. Just a ho-hum 66 and low round of the tournament. It looks like he'll be in the final pairing tomorrow with Colin Montgomerie (72-67). And to think, Woods started the tournament with a 40 on the front nine Thursday.

At the end of the day I adjourned to the patrons parking lot to join Arnold Palmer and friends at The Colonel's tailgate party. The Colonel has been coming to The Masters since 1956, and Arnie (well, it's actually a life-size cutout of Arnie from a Cooper Tires promotion) comes every year, too. I had my picture taken with "Arnie," so I get points for that, and I met Eddie Heimann, the tailor who designed the original Green Jacket worn by Augusta members and Masters winners (more points.) It was a great party. Right there in the parking lot as thousands of spectators walked by, I was hangin' out with Arnie and the boys. Rob Gillette, Howdy Giles (1994 Golf Nut of the Year) and fellow Registered Golf Nut Pete Richter (#2072) were there, along with their wives. There were several other "golf nut" types there as well. It was the perfect way to end my first day at my first Masters.

After the tailgate party we adjourned to the house we had rented for the week and ordered pizza (Pizza Hut Thin & Crispy, thank you very much). After our gourmet meal we all jumped into two cars and followed Rob to the house Ben Crenshaw had rented, where Rob presented him with a beautiful magnum-size bottle of wine specially engraved to commemorate Ben's 1996 Old Tom Morris Award. All I can say after meeting Ben this evening is that he is one of those rare individuals who is even nicer in person than he seems to be on television. What a credit to the game of golf.

After the visit with Ben we all went home to watch USA Network's telecast of the day's play. I was so tired that I fell asleep in my chair while watching John Huston make a 10 on the 13th. I had slept only two hours since Wednesday night, and it finally caught up with me. In fact, I slept in until 10:30 the next morning, when I could have been at The Masters. I should be impeached.

4/12/97 - Actually, sleeping in until 10:30 a.m. this morning wasn't exactly a felony, since the first tee time was 10:45 a.m., with Tiger Woods not teeing off until 2:03 p.m. We all showered and dressed, and headed for The Magic Kingdom of Golf for Day Two of our excellent adventure. Breakfast was at the course, and was the traditional egg salad sandwich wrapped in green paper. Price: $1 each. I had three. Lunch was the totally awesome pimento cheese sandwiches for which The Masters has become famous, also $1.

The concession stands at Augusta are unbelievable. Not only is the food incredibly affordable, but also the system is the most efficient I've ever seen. You get in one of four single-file lines at one of the several concession stands on the grounds (they're green, of course.) As you move through the line, the food selections are presented to you on shelves at a 45-degree angle in open crate-like containers. As you near the end of the line, you select the drink you want from a series of young volunteers whose job it is to fill cups with beer (lite or regular) or soft drinks. As you pass, you pick up your favorite beverage and go to one of six cashiers. The line moves very fast, but don't make the mistake of asking for napkins. There aren't any. I learned that one the hard way when I asked the friendly cashier where the napkins were. "You'll find those out on Washington Road at McDonald's or Shoney's," she replied with a wry smile. I could tell she'd used that line more than once before I showed up. I guess the Masters folks decided that white napkins wouldn't look very good on television—and then decided that green napkins wouldn't look very good either. Makes sense to me.

I watched some of Crenshaw's round on Saturday before returning to the big oak tree on the hill near the first tee to watch Woods tee off with his three shot lead over Montgomerie. As I was waiting for Tiger's tee time, I ran into Howdy Giles again. He introduced me to Bert Harbin, who rented his home to Arnie in 1964, and for the next 18 years became a personal friend of Arnie's in the process. In fact, Bert had cooked breakfast for him yesterday before Arnie left town (Nut points!). By the time the round with Tiger Woods was over, Montgomerie was considering another line of work. Tiger surgically removed any chance of Monty winning the tournament by shooting 65 to Montgomerie's 74. I watched every one of those 65 shots, and it was unbelievable. This kid is going to be around for a long time. In fact, here's the bet I'll give anyone who wants it: I'll take Tiger Woods in every major championship (Masters, U.S. Open, British Open, and PGA Championship) for the next 20 years, and you can choose any player you want in each one of those majors. I think I'll win more often than I'll lose. Here, in my humble opinion, is what makes him so good:

1. He hits it consistently 30 to 60 yards longer than everybody else.
2. He also hits it straight.
3. He can hit the tee shot that is called for on a given hole (e.g., fade or draw).
4. He has distance control and trajectory control on his iron shots.
5. He has accuracy with his irons.
6. He is a very good putter, especially on the 3- to 10-footers.
7. He has excellent game management discipline.
8. He has an incredibly strong belief system. He doesn't just believe he can win, he believes he should win.
9. He plays fearlessly, or at least shows no fear when he plays.

It was an incredible experience watching him hit the shot that was called for, shot after shot, hole after hole. Despite the conventional wisdom that Augusta National favors a golfer who can hit a draw, it actually requires the ability to hit it both ways, and Tiger hit what was required on every hole, whether he was hitting a tee shot or an approach. And he always took the aggressive route. After the round, Mark Barnard (Rob's friend who stayed in the rental house with me) and I stayed to watch some of the players on the driving range. We were able to see Bernhard Langer, Tom Kite, Lee Janzen, Davis Love, Lee Westwood and, of course, Woods, who closed down the range (Nut points for Tiger).

Not to be outdone, Mark and I found a driving range that stayed open until midnight, and we closed that place down after dinner (Nut points for us). The balls were really bad, but after watching The Masters, we had to hit *something*.

4/13/97 - Sunday, the final round of The Masters. Woods has a nine shot lead. The only way he can lose is if he gets lost on the way to the course. I decided the only thing that made sense today was to follow Tiger for his entire round, regardless of how many thousands of people were following him. I'm fairly tall (6-3) and can stand behind most crowds and see pretty well. And besides, Augusta National is the birthplace of spectator golf (or is that "patrons" golf? Oh well, you know what I mean). Watching a golf tournament on this golf course is the most pleasant experience a golf spectator could ever have. The land has lots of naturally elevated areas as well as spectator mounding that makes it quite easy for the patrons to see plenty of action, even when it's a large number of fans following Tiger.

Since Tiger didn't tee off until 3:08 p.m., I decided to just stand near the big oak up by the first tee, watch the players tee off, and enjoy the crowd. I also had a suspicion that Howdy Giles, 1994 Golf Nut of the Year, might also wander by, since this was also a favorite spot of his. I hadn't been stationed at my outpost for more than 20 minutes when "The Mayor," as they call him around there, appeared. As Tiger's tee time approached, I moved up the first fairway to stay a little ahead of the huge crowd that would obviously be following him. On the first drive, Montgomerie out drove him by five yards. Tiger, of course, had hit 3-wood and Montgomerie driver.

My strategy throughout the round was to alternate between getting a close-up of a tee shot and being down the fairway from the approaches. It worked pretty well, as I was able to see virtually all of the approaches and most of the drives. When I couldn't get a good close-up of Tiger on the tee, I would head down the fairway to see where he drove it, and then go up near the green as the golfers were walking to their drives.

As I was standing near the par-3 fourth green waiting for Tiger to hit his approach, I got a strong indication of his star power. There in the crowd, craning to catch a glimpse of Tiger Woods was none other than Jack Nicholson. I had heard he was a golf nut, so I introduced myself as The Head Nut of the Golf Nuts Society and gave him an application. He looked at the card, and then at me, with that strange look that made him instantly famous in *Easy Rider* so many years ago and said, "Golf Nuts Society. I'm qualified."

He thanked me, and put the application in his pocket along with my card. I'm sure I'll never hear from him. However, later that day I mentioned my chance meeting with Jack Nicholson to Howdy Giles, and "The Mayor" told me that a good friend of his, John Bannon, was also a friend of Jack's. I gave Howdy an application for John and asked him to see if John could also recruit Nicholson. I think I may have also bribed Howdy with bonus points too, but "I can't recall." Jack Nicholson would be a fine addition to our small band of rebels.

Howdy made some history today at The Masters. Dave Elliott, an Augusta native, asked Howdy for his daughter's hand in marriage. As it turned out, Dave's parents were at The Masters and I was given the honor of taking a picture of Howdy and Carolyn and the Elliotts on this special occasion. Howdy gets a ton of Nut points for that one.

Howdy and Carolyn joined me as I watched Tiger play Amen Corner. As we were following Tiger on 10, Howdy saw Dan Forsman in the gallery. He knows Dan as a former winner of the Bay Hill Invitational, and Howdy introduced me. Dan is a very nice man who looks you right in the eye when introduced to you, conveying a genuineness that is refreshing in a celebrity/athlete of his stature. Dan played in this year's Masters, but missed the cut. He was enjoying the round as a spectator, showing a friend around the course. He's obviously an excellent candidate for membership in the Society.

As the round progressed, the crowd grew. And as Tiger moved to 17-under for the tournament with a two-putt birdie from 15 feet on the 13th, they were all in his corner as he attempted to break the 72-hole record held jointly by Jack Nicklaus and Ray Floyd. He needed one more birdie. It didn't take long. On the 14th hole, Tiger followed up a perfect tee shot with a low, checking wedge that spun to a stop 10 feet below the hole. After his putt hit the bottom of the cup, he had the all-time low tournament score, if only he could finish at that number.

On 15, his tee shot was in the right rough, but he hit it so far that he actually had to hit a fade in order to negotiate a small group of tall pines that were about 100 yards short and right of the green. He cut the shot a bit too much and "short-sided" himself, leaving a very difficult chip. As it turned out, he had to make a 10-foot putt for par after running his birdie putt well past the hole, which isn't hard to do at The Masters (Stimpmeter reading: 12). On 16, he executed the stroke of the century to two-putt from the top shelf, 35 feet from the hole. His ball nearly stayed on the top shelf, but it was hit with the exact speed necessary to stop near the hole.

On 17, he drove the ball so far he had to take a drop from the spectator crosswalk. His sand wedge was perfect, but the pin had been placed on an "army helmet" in the back right section of the green, and his ball trickled to the fringe after almost stopping 10-feet from the hole. Two putts later, he needed a par on 18 to establish a new 72-hole record.

After Tiger hit his approach putt to within three feet of the hole on 17, I walked to the back of the 18th tee to witness history. And as it turned out, I almost witnessed a disaster. I was standing under the television tower, watching Tiger take his backswing, when I heard the distinctive click and whir of a high-speed auto-wind camera. As I recall, it went off twice during Tiger's swing. As history will note, Tiger's drive was a huge snap-hook. Tiger whirled and glared at the tower where two still photographers stood in a state of semishock.

Each photographer had a camera in hand, and a third camera was attached to the tower. One of the photographers shook his head "no" as he pointed to the camera attached to the tower, seeming to say that this was the camera that went off. I felt for the photographers, since they would never do anything like that intentionally at a time like this, and I felt for Tiger, who was trying to make history. Fortunately, Tiger is so long that his snap-hook missed the trees on the left and was wide open with just over 100 yards to the green.

The ensuing scene provided a light-hearted moment for the spectators who had been lining the left side of the fairway. They formed what could be loosely described as a 100-yard long procession line for Tiger as he approached his ball, everyone hooting and cheering. He smiled and seemed to really enjoy the adulation and levity as he walked toward his ball. And as we all know, he knocked his ball onto the green and two-putted from about 30 feet above the hole for the victory, the record, and pretournament favorite status at The Masters for the next 20 years. It was an awesome sight to behold, as I stood behind the 18th green watching this incredible scene unfold. I had witnessed history in my first Masters.

I stayed for the presentation ceremony, and it was definitely worth the wait. On the practice putting green, facing the setting sun, representatives from every golf association in the world were seated alongside the green-jacketed members of Augusta National Golf Club. At the front of this large group was a cherry wood table, behind which Jack Stephens, President of Augusta National, and Will Nicholson, Chairman of the Tournament Committee, sat in large cherry wood chairs. Alongside the table were two more chairs. Woods sat in one, and Nick Faldo, the previous year's champion, sat in the other.

On the table was the champion's trophy, a silver replica of the large silver permanent trophy. The champion also receives a gold medal, which was on the table. And, of course, lying on the table was the famous green jacket, symbolic of victory and honorary membership in the Augusta National Golf Club. Twenty-five feet in front of this group was a row of perhaps 50 photographers and cameramen from around the world. The members of the representing golf associations were introduced. The members of Augusta National Golf Club were acknowledged as a group, and Will Nicholson gave an eloquent and brief presentation speech.

Tiger spoke for about 10 minutes, thanking those who had contributed to his victory: his parents, the fans, Lee Elder, Charlie Sifford. He was then whisked away to the media room in a golf cart surrounded by a small army of Pinkerton guards. As the cart moved down the hill past the big oak tree, a small boy of perhaps six or seven years of age was running alongside the cart yelling "Goodbye, Tiger" to the hero he could not see. Being a bit taller than this small fan, I was able to see Tiger turn and smile in the direction of the young voice.

It was obvious that Tiger has an abiding love for children, and they can sense it. He is their hero, and I believe that he will be a fine role model for them. I walked over to the young boy and told him that Tiger had smiled at him when he heard the boy say "goodbye." He beamed a huge smile and seemed to walk taller as he and his mother left the tournament grounds. He had connected with his hero, and life was good.

After the awards presentation, I drove to Bert Harbin's daughter's home for a post-tournament party of chicken wings and seafood gumbo. I don't do chickens, but I sure did enjoy that seafood gumbo. Howdy Giles was there, and we all talked about the tournament and what a wonderful week it had been. Howdy was kind enough to allow me to spend the night at the home he and his wife had rented for the week, since I had had to vacate my rental by noon Sunday.

4/14/97 - I was up at 6:00 this morning and off to the airport, but first Howdy and I had to rendezvous at a Krispy Kreme donut shop to get some fresh, hot donuts (a Masters tradition) and buy every *Augusta*

Chronicle newspaper we could find. I bought four donuts and a dozen newspapers. The headline was perfect. It was one word:

"HISTORIC!"

That kind of says it all doesn't it? The demand was so high for copies of that issue that this was the first time in Masters history the *Augusta Chronicle* had to do a reprint of their Monday issue. I should have gotten two dozen.

As I headed out of town, down Interstate 20 toward Atlanta and my return flight to Phoenix, the early morning sun was peeking over the tree-tops. I was listening to a local Augusta radio station, and "Oh Augusta," the official Masters theme began playing. I'm not ashamed to admit I had tears rolling down my cheeks as the song played. It was the perfect ending to a perfect weekend in Augusta. I can't wait to go back.

MY DAY AT THE MASTERS
By Jim Whittemore (Nut #1746)

When I got a last minute call from Dave Lobeck, President and COO of Fuzzy Zoeller Productions, inviting me to the 2000 Masters I shook it off as being too last minute, can't do it, got too much on my plate and every other excuse I could think of. The guilt pangs lasted for about three minutes. I called him back and said, O.K. I'm there. Dave's response was, "Get your ass to Louisville Sunday and we'll fly down on Bogey Bird."

How good was this? Three days at the Masters with Fuzzy, who I had befriended 16 years ago as his host at the Fred Meyer Challenge Pro-Am at Astoria Country Club. Dave and I had become good friends since the day he started running Fuzzy's company.

Since that summer of '86, suffice it to say that Fuzzy and I have shared a lot of laughs, a few tears, and a gentlemanly amount of barleycorn. He has been there for me throughout Amateur qualifiers ("Quit lookin' at the scoreboard, Whittemore") and proudly, I for him. A great friendship has endured through it all.

My brother-in-law, Craig Honeyman, and I took the red-eye to

Louisville via DFW and checked into a downtown hotel to freshen up and grab a bite to eat. Lobeck picked us up and 10 minutes later we were loading luggage on Bogey Bird.

We were met at the airport and taken to the course to pick up Fuzzy's courtesy car. Augusta National met us with a larger than normal vehicle to stop by the course (notice how natural this is sounding) and pick up our courtesy car. Fuzzy knows I am in seventh heaven and asks the driver to take us down Magnolia Lane, not the back entrance. I've died and gone to heaven. This is it. The Holy Grail.

We pick up the car, get settled in at the house, and then head to T-Bones for dinner. I couldn't pay the check fast enough. Traveling with Fuzzy, you've got to stay a step ahead. His generosity has no limits. I gave my credit card to the hostess when we arrived and I told her in no uncertain terms, I am buying dinner. A twenty-dollar bill sealed the deal.

The next day, Monday, I got my first look at the Shrine. But Fuzzy, as usual, had something up his sleeve. As we were walking toward the front door of the clubhouse, Fuzzy said, "Hey Whitts, come with me. Guys, we'll see you in a bit."

I have no idea where we're going. Then he asked, "Want some breakfast?"

"Sure," I said or some other unintelligible acknowledgment. Next thing I know he was leading me upstairs to the Champions locker room. We sat down with Craig Stadler and his brother and had a very relaxing 45-minute breakfast. We didn't talk golf, but bird hunting. What else do you talk about with two Masters champions in the most exclusive locker room in the world? Made sense to me. Of course, I ordered basted eggs, which according to Brandel Chamblee are the specialty of the house. And that they were.

Magnolia Lane. Champions Locker Room. The inside of the clubhouse, for God's sake. And I still hadn't seen the golf course. We finished breakfast, Fuzzy signed a few flags, changed his shoes and we headed to the practice tee.

How's my day going? I was determined to photograph every hole at

Augusta. Eighty exposures later, mission accomplished. The galleries—excuse me, the patrons—at Augusta are the kindest, most polite and knowledgeable anywhere. I have managed my share of professional golf tournaments and these are the most gracious people I have ever met. Many times throughout the day I would ask to get a shot, and these people would part the waters, especially when they found out it was my first visit to Augusta.

As we were making the turn, I heard Fuzzy on the 10th tee yell to Lobeck. "Where's Whittemore?"

"Make sure he goes down the right side of the fairway, not the left."

The previous night Fuzzy remarked that the 10th at Augusta is the most beautiful hole in golf. And he played it like he loves it. He blew his tee shot past Herron, Huston, and Daly. Not bad for an ol' man.

Television does not do it justice. It is that spectacular. A huge golf hole. Honeyman and I made our way down 10, over the hill on 11, and finally to the 12th tee. I could not believe the amount of ground this little par 3 consumed. The expanse of land at Augusta is still hard to fathom, but the 12th hole is one of the biggest par 3s in the world. Bleachers and grass seating can accommodate more than 10,000 patrons, on a par 3, no less.

Absolutely breathtaking. As the group leisurely made its way over from the 11th green I was frantically taking pictures of the 12th hole. Long lens, wide angle, and the whole thing. Then I got a shot of Fuzzy walking up to the tee. How he picked me out of 10,000 people I'll never know.

I finally heard, "Hey Whittemore get down here."

I froze. This isn't happening. I motion to Fuzzy and sort of wave him off and move back up to my seat on the grass. He calls out again and then the crowd gets into it. They were egging me on. No choice. I moved through the crowd, down the bank and under the ropes. Fuzzy bent over and teed up a ball. "OK, pardsie, let's see what you got."

This is perfect. I've been challenged by the "master" to tee it up in front of 10,000 people on the hardest par 3 in all of golf. The shakes begin. And then I don't know what took over. Was it divine intervention, or Mom and Dad looking down from their celestial balcony? I calmly walked over to his bag, pulled out a 7-iron and started making practice swings. Then I had the gall to pull his glove out of his back pocket and put it on. Why not?

Bernhard Langer was up on the green practicing for what seemed like an eternity. Fuzzy was motioning to the crowd, pointing to the right with a slow waving motion. All the while, a guy in the crowd was capturing everything on video. Yes, this entire slow motion, out-of-body experience was being permanently recorded.

Finally Langer finished and Fuzzy stepped back. In his loudest voice he announces: "Ladies and gentlemen, from Portland, Oregon, Jim Whittemore." Herron, Huston, and Daly couldn't believe their eyes.

I had taken a few practice swings and was now really concerned if I could even get it airborne. Then it started. My hands started shaking. And I mean shaking. They were shaking so bad I heard Fuzzy's caddie clearly say, "My God. Look at that. He can't take it back."

And at that moment, somehow I got the club back, hit it as hard as I could and actually walked through the shot. It got airborne all right, and I heard a bit of crowd swell behind me. The ball was in the air and actually heading for the green. The crowd was on its feet and starting to cheer as it came down. The ball landed on the green about 20 feet from the hole. And there was no other way to say it. They went wild. They told me later it was the loudest cheer of the day.

Fuzzy clapped, threw his head back and laughed that hearty laugh. Huston came over and gave me a hug. And there was Daly with the high fives and the biggest grin since Crooked Stick. Eric, Fuzzy's caddy, wrapped his arms around me and had to help me take the glove off, my hands were shaking so bad. Fuzzy gave me a kick in the pants and I headed back to my seat.

The rest of the day was a blur. The congratulations and "attaboys" were nonstop. People being so nice, saying hello, shaking my hand, even taking pictures. And it was all for one swing on the greatest hole in golf.

When the day was over we headed home and changed for dinner. As we loaded up in the courtesy car, Phil Lobeck, Dave's brother, came around to the side door and saw me sitting by the window. Even though I was still in a fog, nobody ever wants to sit in the middle seat, right? He gave me one look and said, "Move over dammit. You've had a pretty good day." I gladly sat in the middle. I played the 12th hole at Augusta.

Thanks, Fuz.

THE KING
By Scott Houston (Nut #1186)

(Editor's note: Scott Houston [Nut #1186] is a full-time caddie at Pebble Beach, and has had the good fortune of caddying for Arnold Palmer several times. On one occasion Arnie "stiffed" a 7-iron on Pebble's 18th hole, and instead of replacing the divot that Arnie made, Scott kept it. He planted it in a flowerpot that he keeps at his home. *Sports Illustrated* did a story about it. Here are two short stories—from Scott's perspective—about his experiences with The King. The first is about caddying two days for Palmer, and the second about Arnie's final Masters round).

Just finished two days with THE KING at Pebble. It's just too difficult for words. I don't possess the vocabulary to describe the presence, the effect, and the graciousness; that "I told you so" grin when he hits a remarkable or "called" shot. The look he gets while preparing for a shot with no resignation to age.

The word spreads around Pebble that "He" is playing. At 14 green eight people are waiting; at 15 green, twenty-five; at 16, thirty-some. At 17 tee I've got to push my way through the crowd, and everyone walks 18 behind or to the side of him. Just remarkable.

One can feel the crowd's energy. They want to applaud. They want to touch him, call his name. They are in awe of his presence. And then a young mother walks out of the crowd and asks Arnie to sign the sneaker of her two-year-old girl. And, of course, he signs it, with a smile. And then someone in the gallery, who recognizes the fact that I'm Arnie's caddie, asks me if it's okay to approach him.

"Approach Mr. Palmer?"

"How many moments will you have in your life to do so? Of course it's OK. He's THE KING. It's your moment, and the man makes moments."

I could go on...How, when I'm not attentive on the green and he wants the ball cleaned, he'll put it behind his back and wait with cupped hand by his side for me to return it. And if I'm late to do so, he fires a low and outside fastball at me from up to 10 feet away! I love him.

I'm not an icon worship sort of guy, but Mr. Palmer is special and I'm honored to have discussed any increment of golf strategy, yardage, etc. with him. He is The King. Forget about the golf resume, his credentials as just "Arnie" surpass all those birdies.

P.S.: I showed Arnie the *SI* piece about the divot, and he LAFFFFFFFFFFFFFFFFFED!!

(A good friend of Arnie's told me that secretly, Arnie loves the divot!!!) He signed the *SI* piece to Bill and Karen, my parents, and one to me: "To Scott, good job, Arnold Palmer." So now I have a special Arnie collection going. I'll never wash the towel that cleaned his clubs. He gave me a pin from his bag (his "umbrella" logo). I have his ball with the same umbrella, the divot, a couple of photos (one with Clint Eastwood, Arnie, and me) and an autograph on a Pebble scorecard. And, of course, I hope the collection grows.

*****

Just read an Arnie interview while watching him play the 12th at Augusta National. I had tears in my eyes. I'm watching the faces on the "patrons" as he walks by; they're all smiling. I'm watching his face, the lines, the smile, the eyes, how he holds the ball and tee together prior to puttin' 'em in the ground and I'm thinkin' how fortunate, no, how blessed I am to have spent hours with this man. I've caddied for arguably the most popular golfer ever and I'm not too sure about that, but I'm certain Arnie possesses the greatest character of any golfer ever.

Unless you've walked and talked with this man, unless you've watched how he treats people and feel the love that's returned, it's very difficult to describe. I'll share this with you: The first time I met and caddied for Arnie at Pebble...throughout the day it's, "Ok, what's this playin'?" . . . "What have you got for me now Scott?" . . . "Okay pro, what do you think?". . .

And then in the middle of 16 he looks me in the eye and says, "Okay, Scott Houston, what's this playin'?" And I looked back, speechless.

"That is your name—Scott Houston, isn't it?"

"Yes sir, Mr. Palmer, but you remembered my entire name."

"We were introduced on the first tee weren't we Mr. Houston?"

"Yes sir, Mr. Palmer, we were. You've got 146 center, 137 front and 152 to the pin."

"Let's hit the seven," he replied.

And of course he knocked it close, just like you want him to, every time.

But who hasn't the man met? Presidents. Kings. Queens. And even at age sixty-nine, has the decency to remember someone's name.

I was not "just a caddie," and Arnold Palmer is not just another golfer. He is THE KING.

"I pulled it!"

16th Hole

"I HATE THIS GAME!"

Okay, I'll admit it. I could really go "nuclear" in my early years. There, I feel better already.

Hey, I'm not alone, you know. Bobby Jones was a real "pistol" in his early days, and we've all heard the famous Tommy Bolt stories. Even Tiger Woods has a temper (remember his famous "blue streak" of invective after he snapped off a drive into the blue Pacific in the 2000 U.S. Open?). And who can ever forget the priest in *Caddyshack?* If the game can drive a man of God to the 19th Hole, what chance do the rest of us have?

I don't know what it is about this game that drives me nuts. Maybe it's the huge difference between the feeling of a great shot and a lousy shot that sends me into my Jekyll and Hyde routine. All I know is that when I hit a bad one, I just want to find something to gnaw on. I swear (yes, I did: and a lot!) that there is nothing more irritating than a chunked chip, unless it's a bladed long iron.........or a shanked wedge........or a topped drive.........or...........or...........or.........God, I hate this game. (Sometimes.)

I'm ashamed to admit there was a time in my golf career when I never had a full set of clubs in my bag. One was always in the repair shop getting reshafted after I had snapped it over my knee. Admittedly, there's something very therapeutic about rendering a golf club useless after it has disobeyed.

Which reminds me of my longtime love, my Zebra putter. Back when the Zebra first came on the market I bought the first one that came into the pro shop, and I putted with that putter for over 10 years. We made such sweet music together for such a long time, I couldn't believe it when she decided to "retire." I didn't understand it at all. She just stopped making putts. It started with those little short, left-to-right three- and four-footers. They used to be automatic. For 10 years she made nearly every single one she looked at, and then it stopped. She started missing them to the right. I mean, she didn't even hit the hole. It was sad to watch that old putter lose her touch.

One day, after one too many missed three-footers, I just stood up from my putt, held her in both hands—one hand on the grip end and one hand on the putter head—looked at her lying there in front of me, and bid her farewell. Goodbye, Lady Zebra. I broke her in half. Then I took what was left and broke her in half again. No remorse. I put the head in the attic with my other defective clubs, just in case she called out to me someday, to claim she had mended her ways.

A few weeks later I began having feelings of guilt. Was it all her fault? Or was I perhaps partially responsible for some of those missed putts? I pulled her out of the attic and took her to a trophy shop and had a plaque made of her remains. It was the least I could do. We had had some good years together. That was 14 years ago. I still have the plaque.

Just the other day I ran into a guy at the golf course who was putting with one of those old original Zebras, just like my "Lady Zebra," so I asked him if I could hit a putt with it, you know, for old times' sake. I rolled it right in the jar from about 10 feet. The next day I went to Uinta Golf to see if they had an old used Zebra hanging around, and sure enough they did. I bought it, and I've been putting with it ever since. Go figure.

Not long after the "Lady Zebra" incident, I asked the pro at our club if I could try a set of his personal irons on the premise that I might like to buy a set like them from his pro shop. He agreed, and I went out to the front nine with these new blades, excited about the prospect of them holding "The Secret." Before I could make it to the turn, I lost control after a bad shot, slammed one of his clubs into the ground, and broke the shaft.

I felt terrible, and needless to say, it was a very embarrassing moment when I returned the clubs to the pro. Of course, I paid for the reshaft, but that wasn't the point. It was clearly one of the low points of my golf career. I learned my lesson. That was the last club I ever broke.

I've tried just about everything to help me keep my emotional equilibrium when I'm out in the 18-hole torture chamber, but nothing ever provided a permanent cure. However, there were a few interesting temporary fixes that I came up with over the years. There was the "eat the tee" strategy that I developed almost by accident many years ago after hitting yet another tee ball into the trees.

As the ball was making a beeline for the forest, I angrily pulled the tee out of the ground and gently placed it between my teeth while still holding its head in my hand, and ripped it in half. To be honest, it was pretty therapeutic. Over time, the strategy developed to the point where I would just keep chewing until I had pulverized the tee before I would spit it out of my mouth. I haven't taken the extreme step of actually eating the tee, but it has crossed my mind from time to time, especially after a particularly pitiful tee shot.

Mike Hamilton (Nut #0128) developed an interesting variation on this theme many years ago in a match in the California State Amateur. Faced with a sand wedge shot to the green, he "laid the sod over" his pitch, picked up the divot—stared at it—and ate it! Well, I don't know if he actually swallowed the grass and dirt, but he got so torqued that he angrily chewed that divot to pieces (Hey, Mike, don't forget to replace your divot).

Speaking of laying the sod over a sand wedge shot, a few years ago in a tournament I did just that and was so infuriated that I took a mighty swing at the toe of my shoe to relieve a little of the stress. Only one problem; I missed. Instead, I smacked myself right in the shin with the blade of the sand wedge. I guess you might call it a "cut shot," because I started bleeding like a stuck pig. It was a real "gusher!" I almost passed out from the pain, too. I thought I was going to have to withdraw and go to the hospital for stitches, but fortunately, the girlfriend of one of the players in my group had a couple of pretty big Band-Aids. We were able to squeeze the wound together enough to stem the flow of life-giving blood, and I played on to the finish. To add to my embarrassment, one of the guys in our group made a double-eagle on the hole and I missed it because I was busy writhing on the ground in pain while trying to keep from bleeding to death.

Doug Skille (#0186) could snap a club with the best of them. One Saturday afternoon he and I were playing a best-ball match against a couple of fellow members at the club. Skille was standing over a shot of about 200 yards for his second to the par-5 10th hole when he asked me, "Gar, what do you think? A 3-iron or an 8-iron?"

"A 3-iron or an 8-iron! What are you talking about?"

"Well, that's all I've got, said Skille. "I broke my 4, 5, 6, and 7-irons."

"Well, it sure isn't a 3-iron!" I fired back.

He went with the 8-iron and knocked it on. Skille was strong. Very strong.

But my favorite club-breaking story comes by way of Gary Vandeweghe (Nut #2829), who shared the following story about a friend who also fell out of love with his putter. It happened one Wednesday evening at dinner. He was sitting at the table after a day at the office, thinking about his lousy putting that past weekend. In the middle of the meal, he gets up, goes into the garage, grabs his putter from his bag, and snaps it over his knee. Bang. Gone. Broken into two pieces. He drops it on the floor, goes back and finishes dinner. Sleeps well that night too. Now that's nuts, but we at the Society understand completely. Sometimes the game just does that to you.

Feeling (rightfully) that my emotions were holding me back as a player, I decided it was time for radical measures, so I bought a Sony Walkman. Armed with my favorite music, I started playing and practicing with headphones on and my Walkman blaring in my ears. I even went so far as to wear them in golf tournaments. But that didn't work out very well. At one tournament I kept turning the music up louder and louder after every bogey, and on one hole, after everyone had teed off, I started walking down the fairway. One problem; everyone hadn't teed off. There was still one of our foursome on the tee, and my group was trying to get my attention. Peter Moore (#0002) was in the pairing, and he started calling to me:

"Garland......Garland."

It wasn't working, so he tried yelling, and the further I walked, the louder he got: "Garland..........Garland.......Garland!"

Finally, he screamed at the top of his lungs, "GARLAND!!"

I heard that one. Boy, was I embarrassed, but I left the Walkman on. I just turned it down a little.

Golf Nut Gregg Guernsey adds this "Walkman" anecdote:

"It involved the Royal Oaks Country Club driving range. I can remember walking up to the driving range and seeing Ron hitting balls. From 75 yards or so I saw some strings hanging down from his head. Now, my first thought was 'that crazy Garland has another swing gizmo with strings to keep his head still......' As I got closer I could see it was a Walkman. The music blaring from the Walkman was from INXS, a band that catered to the high school crowd. Ron, at the time, was 42 years old."

Enough said.

Later in my career I came up with yet another strategy for coping with anger: push-ups. After a bad shot I would adjourn to a nearby cart path and do knuckle push-ups until I calmed down. When that didn't work, I graduated to doing them on the stubs of my wrists. They're easy, actually. They just hurt, which was the point. One small challenge was picking the small pieces of gravel out of my knuckles and the back of my hands. One time, while playing in the Riverside Best-Ball in Portland, I three-putted the difficult par-3 7th for bogey from six feet. I was not happy. I walked calmly to the cart path beside the eighth tee; laid my bag down, and did 40 wrist push-ups. It was an all-time personal best. Rather than go nuclear, I just decided to do push-ups until I calmed down. Obviously, it took a while. When I finally calmed down 40 push-ups later, my arms were like limp noodles. I nearly whiffed my next tee shot. My drive went a grand total of 150 yards. Parred the hole, as I recall.

"Get the net."

That's what Peter Moore said as he stood by calmly, watching me fly into a rage on the 17th green at Royal Oaks Country Club one Saturday morning. As I recall, I wasn't having a particularly good day, and it all finally caught up with me on 17. So as I frothed at the mouth and flailed about, Moore was having fun comparing my behavior to that of the wild animals captured weekly on Marlin Perkins's *Wild Kingdom*. And he wasn't through. Gregg Guernsey (#0005) was also in the foursome, and Peter decided to have a little more fun.

"Gregg will hold Ron down, while Marlin administers the tranquilizer," he quipped.

Now that was a great line, and it was the perfect antidote. We all fell to the ground in hysterics, and I was able to finish the round without further incident—or thoughts of suicide.

"You have to remember this is when we were quite a bit younger and thought we could really play," Moore recalls. "Anyway Ron, like myself, can get rather passionate—heated might be a better way of saying it—on the golf course."

He's right about that. Moore goes through golf bags faster than anyone in golf. When the game finally gets to him, he gives the bottom of his bag a good beating. It invariably destroys the plastic bottom of the bag, and sooner or later he has to buy a new one. They love him in the pro shop. They store extra bags in his favorite color because they know that it's only a matter of time before he'll be in to buy a new one.

What does he say in his defense?

"I can't help it if they don't make golf bags the way they used to. Those bottoms used to be made out of vulcanized rubber. They could really take a beating."

Pretty weak defense, don't you think?

Perhaps a better form of therapy would be what former Oregon Amateur champion Donnell Smith used to do when the game just got to be too much for him. He would get so upset about his putting that he would throw his putter high into the air after missing a putt, then run under it, stand at attention with his hands firmly at his side, and wait for it to come down and hit him on top of his head. I don't think it ever helped him improve his putting, but it sure was entertaining.

Our beloved Prez used a different tactic. He bought himself some rope, tied it into a noose, tied the noose to the crossbeam in his garage, and "hung" any putter that betrayed him. At one time he had over a dozen putters hanging from that noose. One time he tied one to the bumper of his car after a tournament and dragged it all the way home. When he arrived home, all that was hanging from the bumper was the rope and a beat up putter shaft.

Needless to say, the game can get under our skin at times, and here's how some other Nuts found ways to cope with the stress:

Pete Schenk (#0007) - Went camping to get away from the game for a few days, and ended up building a makeshift nine-hole course in the woods. 500 points.

Marty Price (#0038) - After hitting his approach shot into the lake fronting the seventh green the three previous years in the Capitol City Amateur in Salem, Oregon, he walked up to the edge of the lake and threw in a brand new ball before hitting his approach. The golf gods were not amused. He promptly chunked his next shot into the lake. 107 points.

Mike Hamilton (#0128) - Threw his clubs into a lake near the 18th green and quit the game forever, only to dive into the lake later that evening to retrieve the clubs. He was on the tee the next morning. On another occasion he threw his clubs – bag and all – into a ravine after a poorly-played hole. 800 points.

Mike Hamilton (again) (#0128) - Walked the entire length of Sweetwater River (in the river) during a round of golf at Chula Vista Muni, as self-inflicted punishment for hitting a shot into the river early in the round. He would hit a shot, return to the river, walk in the river, get out of the river, walk to his ball, hit the ball, return to the river...until the round had ended. 518 points.

Art Gemmel (#0739) - Has 18 putters in a garbage can in his garage. While he can't stand to putt with them anymore, he can't bring himself to throw them away either. 180 points.

17th Hole

THE SEARCH FOR "THE SECRET"

The search for "The Secret." That is the Society's higher purpose, our mission, our goal, and our dream. The impossible dream, to be exact. We know it's an impossible dream, but we don't accept that. Our intellect says, "Nope, it doesn't exist." Our heart tells us to keep searching. We follow our hearts, mostly because we don't have a brain.

Perhaps this would be a good time to describe this thing we call "The Secret." It's not the meaning of life, but it is the key to unlocking the hidden code of the perfect golf swing, which makes it much more important than the meaning of life. "The Secret" can be a swing key or a golf club; anything that makes us say, "That's it! I'm never going to hit another bad shot for the rest of my life."

We know it's out there. Heck, I've discovered it hundreds of times myself.

You see, that's the problem. "The Secret" has an expiration date. Just like a quart of milk, your swing can go sour at any time, and it usually does so at the worst possible moment. That's why we search so desperately for the real "Secret." You know, the one that doesn't have an expiration date. Yes, we know that it doesn't exist—but then what if it does? Do you know what I mean? No, really. Do you?

It all makes sense to us. If people can spend their entire lives believing in Santa Claus or seeking world peace, we golf nuts can search for "The

Secret." We have just as much chance of discovering it as those other people have in meeting Santa Claus or bringing about world peace; perhaps a better chance. At least I've hit a few perfect shots during my life, but I've never met the real Santa Claus (and I'll know him when I meet him). And I don't hold out much hope for world peace either.

The good news is that someday, I am hopeful, one of our members is going to discover "The Secret," and we'll scoop the world with the news of its discovery. Go Nuts.

My search for "The Secret" has taken me on some pretty interesting journeys. I've shared some of those with you in the earlier chapters, but there are more.

When I was a member of Columbia Edgewater Country Club in Portland many years ago, the driving range was too small to hit drivers, so I had to come up with an alternate plan. I would wait until nearly dark, after everyone had teed off, and then hit drivers down the first fairway. I wasn't very good in those days, and I would spray balls all over the first hole. I had them in the right rough, the left rough, the right trees, the left trees, and every now and then I would even hit one in the fairway.

I would just keep firing those pills all over the lot until well after dark. I can't tell you how many times I was out in the darkness hitting ball after ball into a full moon. Now that I look back on it, it was a pretty cool experience. But then I had to go pick up the balls. That green superintendent must have hated me. There was no way to find them all at night, so the next morning it must have looked like an Easter egg hunt. When he mowed that area of the course I'll bet he was off his tractor more than he was on it.

We finally got a bigger driving range at Columbia Edgewater, but that didn't end my search for "The Secret." Several years—and several hundred swing changes later—it was 1987—a very interesting year indeed for The Head Nut. Having given up temporarily on ever discovering "The Secret," I decided that it was time to graduate to a more dedicated focus on mental and physical health as part of my golf development.

I had heard that martial arts was excellent for improving concentration, physical conditioning, and flexibility, so I signed up for Kung-Fu lessons. This actually turned out to be very good for me. I became stronger, much more flexible, and I learned how to breathe properly, especially under stress. I developed my "Kung-Fu" preshot routine in which I would breathe through my diaphragm (stomach) instead of my chest. This lowered my center of gravity and relaxed my upper body muscles. It was also a tremendous aid to putting under pressure. And it gave my foursome plenty of "ammo" too. I had to suffer the slings and arrows of my friends' abuse, but when a man is on a mission to discover "The Secret," the cackling of the naysayers must not deter him.

Then I purchased a Soloflex weight training machine for my home, to build my golf muscles. That went over real well with Mrs. Nut, since the only place we could put it was in the family room.

The next step to golfing excellence was eliminating sugar and caffeine from my diet to create better emotional stability during the heat of competition (yeah, right). No more candy? No more Coke? I was trading one kind of stress for another.

Now it was time to get serious. The mental game. It's what separates the "big boys" from us hacks, and I was ready. I purchased a visual imagery instruction course, complete with self-hypnosis tapes, to improve my competitive performance. I took the "Golfer's Behavioral Profile System" psychological test to analyze my behavioral tendencies during tournament play (I don't know why I bothered, I already knew I gagged like a maggot when the heat was on).

Not satisfied with self-hypnosis, I signed up for six sessions with a real hypnotist. It didn't help, but I did get some much-needed sleep.

I told you earlier about the Sony Walkman I bought to listen to music with while playing, but I also bought these really cool "alpha wave" tapes that I would listen to while I was beating balls on the range.

All in all, 1987 was a very strange year. All that mental and physical conditioning, and I didn't win a single tournament. The search went on.

The search for "The Secret" invariably takes a dedicated golf nut on a quest for the perfect teacher. I talked earlier about my experiences with Ben Doyle. Many years later I heard about the extraordinary teaching abilities of Mike Austin. Mike is still the holder of the Guinness World Record longest drive of over 500 yards, but after his competitive days he turned to golf instruction.

I tracked him down and bought his video. Then we talked on the phone a few times. Then I bought his training aid, "The Flammer." Then I took the extraordinary step of flying to Southern California to take a two-hour lesson from him. He was a good teacher, but it's been a while since we worked together. About 15 years as I recall, but I do remember two things from that lesson.

The first was his admonition that golf is like any other sport in that you have to "step" before your "throw" the clubhead, just like you do in throwing a baseball or football; or in hitting a baseball with a bat. You must "step" before you throw. The only difference in golf is that you can't actually "step;" you "shift," then "throw."

The other thing I remember involves the "throwing" of the club.

"Imagine that you are holding a chicken by the head," he said, "and your goal is to 'throw' that chicken so hard down at the bottom of your swing that you 'throw' an egg right out of the chicken's . . ." Well, you get the idea.

So in the summer of 1989 I was hooked on Mike Austin and his "Flammer." After being eliminated in the first round of the Oregon Amateur that year I was particularly frustrated and more than a little bit confused, so I called Mike's home as I was driving back from the tournament. His wife answered the phone and notified me that he had had a stroke and was in the hospital. I gave her my condolences and was about to hang up when she said, "You can call him at the hospital if you like."

What the hell, I thought, and asked her for the phone number. Mike answered the phone, and it was obvious from the start that he was under pretty heavy sedation. But I was under greater stress, so I began firing my questions at him. He did well, under the circumstances, but I can honestly say that it is the only time that I've taken a lesson from someone lying in a hospital bed.

As long as we're on the subject of taking lessons, I would be remiss if I didn't mention Dr. Jeff Leinassar (#0009.) "Hi Tech Doc," as we know him here in the Society, will try anything if he thinks it will improve his game, and one of his favorite things to do is to take lessons. When Mike Gove became the new head professional at his home club, Astoria Country Club, "H.T. Doc" was the first member to sign up for a lesson.

Many years before Mike Gove's arrival, Ed Oldfield was the head pro at Astoria, and Jeff was a regular customer. When Ed moved to a course just outside Chicago, Jeff would take a couple of pilgrimages annually to see him. Then "Doc" bought a membership at Troon Golf & Country Club in Scottsdale, AZ, and began taking lessons from its teaching professional.

The last report from "Hi Tech Doc" was a request for bonus points. He had just signed up for the Royal Oaks Invitational in June, and fearing a less than satisfying result in the tournament, he also signed up for a three-day golf school the following week at Semiahmoo in Blaine, WA. Better safe than sorry, I guess. But wouldn't it have been better to take the lessons before the tournament?

"Hi Tech Doc is always searching for The Secret," says Leinassar, referring to himself in the third person. "New and better clubs, flying all over the country to take lessons, member of three clubs, pissed off I can't hit it solid all the time."

More recently, the Doc boasted, "I drove 300 miles one way (five hours) to take a two-hour golf lesson and turned it into three hours. I stayed late to play nine holes with my pro and decided, upon his advice, I needed a new driver and new Mizuno irons with the newest and latest graphite shafts.

"I occasionally love the game with highlights being four-time Oregon Coast Champion, six-time club champion, 1999 Oregon Senior Amateur

Champion, 2001 contestant in U.S. Senior Open. After a long day doing dentistry, pounding balls is still a passion. Keep hoping one of these years as my muscles get older that I might just stumble on the right swing plane!!"

And now to our "All-Time Swing Change Leader,"—or ATSCL as we call him—Ken Hoel (#1231). Ken is in a league by himself. Nobody, and I mean nobody, changes his or her swing as much as this guy. At last count, he averaged six swing changes a week, and he only plays once or twice a week.

Ken and I used to play a lot of golf together, being members of the same club in Arizona. He is one of the most positive, upbeat people you could ever want to be around, and one of the highlights of my week was to tee it up with him just so I could hear his latest swing theory. And believe me, it was different every week.

One Saturday we were on the fourth tee, and Ken is addressing the ball, going through his preshot routine, when I noticed he was having difficulty "pulling the trigger." He was stuck in neutral, and couldn't start the club back. Finally, he stood up and looked at us and said, "I can't swing without a swing key. I need a swing key, any swing key."

Ken is always thinking about his golf swing. He can't help it. One evening he was at home watching television, when he "got it." He jumped up from his chair, grabbed his driver and a golf ball, went into the front yard, looked down the street to make sure there were no cars coming in his direction, and launched a beauty right down the middle. Then he went back into the house and resumed watching television.

"During the late 1970s," Hoel told me, "my business demanded a weekly two-hour commute from Tucson to Phoenix by car. I found that thinking about the perfect golf swing, or more accurately what went wrong the last time I played, made the time go by quickly during these trips. So, for a couple of years, at least, I spent four hours per week thinking of nothing but how to improve my swing.

"When you concentrate on something that hard for that long, you're bound to find an answer, or at least convince yourself you have, and when you have found an answer—especially to the ever-elusive golf swing 'Secret' you must put it to the test immediately. Many times during these trips I would pull off to the side of the freeway—that's I-17, a major four lane route between the two cities—tee up a ball out of my trunk, hide a golf club next to my leg like I was carrying a rifle into a bank robbery, and wait for a break in traffic. Then a quick set up, apply the new experimental swing thoughts—always plural— and blast it down the highway. Next, jump back in the car and see if I could find the ball somewhere farther up the road. I never did see one, but the rest of the trip was filled with excitement and anticipation of my next visit to the driving range, which thankfully was open late into the night because most of my commute was in the dark anyway.

"Ron Garland and I shared many enjoyable years on the practice range at a club in Arizona. We both had a love for the game and we were never afraid to try something new. It was during this time that Ron gave me the title of ATSCL.

"I've tried it all. Some of us can change our swing in a manner that is discernible to other golfers. I have swung like Trevino—drop it at the top, Nicklaus—roll both feet, Woods—roll right forearm over left, Watson—drive the knees, and even what Watson thinks Hogan's secret was—roll left forearm. I played with Freddie's swing for a month or two, have tried Ernie's rhythm almost weekly, and even went a period where everyone said, 'You're swinging like Jim Furyk.' And I was.

"Offhand I can't think of a swing I have not tried to emulate. Sometimes one thought is correcting a fault created by another thought. Letting the head drift back a few inches ala Curtis Strange caused me to lunge forward during the downswing, which was nicely compensated for by playing the ball forward like Moe Norman. Lose one fault, however, and the whole swing unravels like a cheap suit.

"I don't warm up anymore because three or four shots and I start experimenting. The last thing that works gets carried to the first tee, usually with disastrous results. On the course each wayward shot means to scrap the last swing thought and bring out a new one. This can happen even if I'm well into the round and have hit everything perfect up to that point.

"Swing changing is an addiction. I can create a new swing theory while standing on the tee waiting for the group ahead to clear the green. Fast play is my only salvation.

"My right thumb has seen every conceivable spot on the grip of my driver. So has my left thumb for that matter. I almost broke my wrist trying the 'left hand low, inverted right hand' swing with my driver. Some gimmicks are too silly to have any hope. But occasionally others can actually produce a good shot or two. Remember Johnny Miller's WOOD thoughts—Works Only One Day? Mine are often WOOS thoughts because they work for one swing and not the next.

"During my early golfing years—I started playing when I was 37—I thought the solution was to find the perfect swing thought and then follow it for the entire round. To help achieve this goal I wrote tips on strips of white tape and put them on the toes of my golf shoes. 'HEAD' on the left foot and 'DOWN' on the right, was one of my favorites. Then, to be more discreet, I started writing them on the thumb of my golf glove, kind of like cheating at school. My golf bag has been full of notes, some handwritten, some on scorecards—obviously great discoveries made during a round—some printed and some even laminated. Can you imagine how certain I must have been of the validity of a particular swing thought to have laminated it? Those are usually at the bottom of the bag. I even have lists of things that DON'T work. Don't roll your head like David Duval, for example. I tried that during the last few holes one year during the Senior Amateur qualifying.

"The combinations are endless. Consider that there are at least 100 reasonable swing thoughts you could easily compile by looking through old golf magazines. Any one swing could incorporate four or five of these thoughts during the same swing. A set-up thought or two, a backswing thought or two, a downswing thought or two, an impact thought—only time for one here—and a follow-through thought arc average for me. Now divide your list into these five categories. That means there are 20 swing thoughts to choose from at five points during the swing. Simple math tells us that results in 3,200,000 different swing combinations if you only use one thought for each swing segment. Use two or more, start adding your own ideas. The practice range joke at the our club was something like, 'What you working on, Ken, swing number 43A?' To which I would reply: 'Very perceptive but it was 43A sub 6 dot 4.'

"What works and what doesn't? The good news is I'll never know. If I ever did discover 'The Secret' I would surely quit the game. Because that IS the game, you see; looking for that next swing to feel so smooth, sound so solid, and send the ball sailing into a gorgeous arch toward the target. And I experience it at least once, every time I play." Whew.

Here's one final story about Ken: one year he found himself in a play-off for the Senior Club Championship. He and his play-off opponent tied the first hole with bogeys, with Ken three-putting for his. On the second play-off hole, Ken three-putted for bogey again, but won the playoff when his opponent made a double bogey. Ken promptly went into the pro shop and bought a new putter with his winnings.

When it comes to searching for "The Secret," Ken has a whole army of Nuts behind him doing their best to be the first to discover The Holy Grail, and here are a few stories that you may find somewhat unbelievable but not surprising:

Al Schleunes (#1965) - While reading the David Leadbetter book, *The Golf Swing*, he made margin notes throughout the book, then later lined out all of his notes when the swing keys didn't work. 500 points.

Michael Petru (#0490) - Built a house overlooking a 20-acre lake. Practices hitting balls across one corner of the lake, which has helped him get over his fear of hitting over water. The only problem is the joggers who use the trail around the lake. He is considering asking the association to put up a sign warning, "Hard Hat Area - Watch For Falling Golf Balls." 200 points.

Bob Miller (#0677) - While practicing chip shots with a 7-iron in the hallway of his home, he "got hold of one," sending a beautiful screamer through his daughter's bedroom window. She was grounded at the time for breaking the same window a week earlier. 107 points.

Shaughn Belmore (#0504) - Shattered a ceiling light, poked a hole in the ceiling, took a carpet divot, and wiped out a table lamp with a single swing in his mother's living room. 400 points.

Dennis Murphy (#0811) - Overcome by the occasional urge to hit a golf shot, he opens the sliding glass door of his 22nd floor downtown condominium and hits 4-wood shots off the carpet and into the city below. On one occasion, he pulled the shot ever so slightly, the ball striking the doorjamb and rebounding toward Dennis, who ducked just in time. The ball embedded in the wall behind him, and he left it there as a reminder not to pull his tee shots. 224 points.

Robert Marple (#1036) - When practicing putting on the living room rug, he uses the vacuum cleaner to set the rug's "grain" to create left-to-right, right-to-left or straight putts. 150 points.

Lawton Harrison (#1093) - Putts on concrete when preparing for a tournament with fast greens. 100 points.

More Lawton Harrison (#1093) - Plays barefoot so he can "feel the golf course." 200 points.

Lawton Harrison (yet again) (#1093) - Plays with earplugs on occasion so he can appreciate the importance of the sense of hearing during a golf swing. 200 points.

"I'm sorry Mrs. Rose, but I'm afraid your husband is terminally nuts."

18th Hole

THERE IS NO CURE

"I'm sorry, ma'am, but there is no known cure for your husband's condition."

Under other more serious circumstances, those would be pretty ominous words. But when it's Dear Abby talking to a golf widow, it's not quite so serious. Unless you're the golf widow.

You remember the earlier letter to Abby about "Morey." He is living proof that there usually isn't a cure. Which reminds me of another icon, the late Ann Landers. She once reported that a survey had asked men to choose between sex and their favorite athletic activity.

"The results were an education, to say the least," wrote Ms. Landers. "Would you believe that sex came in second with golfers? More golfers said that they would gladly forgo the pleasures of the flesh for the joy of their favorite sport. What's more, the golfers were most adamant in defending their choice," she concluded.

That story is clearly one of the seminal events in the battle of the sexes. It is a clear message to nongolfing spouses that golf is a non-negotiable item on the married golfer's agenda. Golf has ruined marriages, destroyed careers, decimated fortunes, and generally laid waste to more than a few dreams of "someday breaking 80." But we keep playing. We say that we love the game, and then complain that "golf" is the original four-letter word.

It's the ultimate love-hate relationship. We've all quit the game forever more than once, only to come back for more abuse. We can't explain our strange attraction to a game that is at once fulfilling and frustrating and frankly, we don't spend a whole lot of time trying to, either. But we sure love to talk about the game—our game.

We have no compunction about regularly coming home late for dinner and blindly regaling the entire family with the complete, unabridged story of our round, to the point that they fall face first into their mashed potatoes from boredom. What possesses us to think that anyone actually gives a damn about the 7-iron we stiffed out on 17?

We start on the first tee, and then take them for the full ride, no charge. Which reminds me of a great line I heard Oregon golf legend Don Krieger deliver to someone who was recounting his round, shot by shot.

"Wait a minute," Don interrupted. "Am I going to need a cart?"

Thankfully, the "round" ended before they got off the third tee.

We'll play in any kind of weather, too. What's that all about? Are we so addicted to the need to catch one in the center of the clubface that weather is merely a necessary evil, or are we trying to say something about our addiction? By playing in tornadoes and hurricanes and lightning storms and weather colder than an arctic winter are we actually calling out for help? Well, yes and no.

And the money we'll spend to support our habit. I don't know about you, but every time I find it necessary to go into the attic for something, I have to go past all of those clubs that I've thrown up there. I look at them and just scratch my head in amazement. What could have possessed me to buy this club? I will ask myself. And when I don't come up with an answer, I quickly change the subject. Better to be unsure than to be reminded.

I also come up with no answer when pondering why our loved ones would put up with our bizarre behavior. We've played golf on holidays, missed birthdays and anniversaries, played hooky from work, and been threatened with divorce over this maddening game. But we keep playing, and remain married. Well, most of us. Are we just lucky, or is there something about the game that taps into the minds of our spouses and tells them, "Everything is going to be all right. Ron needs to do this to keep from going certifiably insane; let him play." Sometimes I think there is; I really do. What else could it possibly be? Do they really love us that much? I don't think so.

Mrs. Nut has often threatened to start the Golf Widows Society, a support group for forgotten spouses. So far I've been successful in discouraging her. The last thing we golf nuts need is organized opposition. There's a lot of truth to that old concept of strength in numbers. I can imagine huge armies of women marshaling their forces and organizing a "club burning" not unlike the "bra burnings" of the 60s. I shudder at the thought.

Mrs. Nut has been amazing though. During those family vacations that were spent with me playing in tournaments, she would take the kids to amusement parks or museums while I was playing. On a good day we would go out to eat. On bad days, she recalls, I would be grouchy and we would get McDonald's and eat in at the motel.

Somebody recently asked Judy if she played golf. This was her exact answer: "Oh no. No. No. No. I used to play a little but Ron couldn't stand to watch my swing. He said looking at it would mess up his swing. Golf is really kind of a stupid game. It used to dictate every decision we made as a family including where we lived. That's kinda weird. But golf keeps him going. The hi-tech industry in which he works has been very up and down. Golf was his sanity."

I can see it as clearly as the line of a 10-foot putt for the club championship. Millions of angry wives taking up arms against us, stealing our clubs while we sleep, and slipping away to a midnight bonfire at the local chapter of the Golf Widows Society to throw our sticks on the fire. Perhaps we should be grateful that they don't grab one of our clubs and beat us to death. Which reminds me of a great joke:

The local police department receives a phone call from a woman who, in a calm voice, says, "My husband is dead. He's lying in bed, and he's been clubbed to death."

The police quickly dispatch an investigator to the scene. When the officer arrives, the woman greets him and takes him to the bedroom, where the victim is lying in a pool of blood on the bed. The officer walks over to the body, and notices a bloody golf club lying on the bed next to the victim.

He inspects the scene, then turns to the woman and says, "Ma'am, it looks like he's been hit seven or eight times with that 5-iron."

"Put me down for a five," the woman calmly replies.

Yes, we golf nuts are lucky. Lucky that our spouses put up with us, and lucky to be alive.

Speaking of luck, one of the most puzzling things to me about our disease is our eternal optimism. We can play an entire round as though we've never held a club in our hands before, but on virtually every shot throughout the entire round, we are absolutely convinced that this shot—the next shot—will be "the shot of the century." Where do we get that optimism?

One of the funniest things about golf is listening to the post-round comments at the 19th Hole.

"I hit it right in the middle of the fairway on seven, and then dumped it in the drink on my approach. Made triple."

"Yeah, well check this out. I knocked it four feet from the hole on 13 and three putted."

"You want to talk three-putts? I had six of 'em today."

"You guys don't know misery. I had three four-putts on the front nine alone."

"Geez, if I putted that bad, I'd quit."

"Well, I would, but I really enjoy the game."

And that's the way we talk, week after week, round after round. Why are we so optimistic? I guess we're just nuts.

Another thing that puzzles nongolfers is how we can sit and watch televised golf for hours. One day my daughter's boyfriend walked through the living room and said, "I don't understand why anyone would watch golf."

"I don't know, I guess because we like it," was all I could come up with. Then I added, "We also like to watch the pro's technique, since we're always trying to improve."

"That makes sense," he said, and left the room, which is what most non-golfers do when golf is on television.

We do spend an awful lot of time and money searching for "The Secret." And we're not shy about practicing at every opportunity. We can't pass a picture window without taking a practice swing with an imaginary club. Doesn't matter if we're in a three-piece suit in downtown Manhattan. If the urge strikes, we do it. You know those elevators that have mirrors on the walls? I love those things. Anytime I'm in one alone, I check my swing. You get both angles at once—front view and side view. It is a bit embarrassing, though, when the elevator door opens and you're in mid-swing. I've gotten some very strange looks, and they're usually in a hurry to get out of the elevator too. What, me "nuts?" Nah.

Anyway, you get the point. We golfers are a strange group. My wife thinks it's a mental disorder, but I know better. It's a disease, and it's contagious. All you need to do is hit just one good shot, and you're hooked for life. You might quit "forever," but it's a temporary condition. You'll be back. Nobody quits "forever" forever. We're all hooked on a feeling. Ben Hogan once said that the feeling of a perfectly struck shot comes up through the shaft, into your hands, and into your heart. It's better than sex. Trust me.

I told that to a thirty-something guy one day after I hit a perfect drive, and he looked at me funny and said, "Then you must be doing something wrong."

And I said, "No, Mike, you've just never hit one that good."

We're hooked on that feeling—and the sense of power we feel when we are able to control such a small object over such a long distance. We're hooked on the technical demands, aesthetic beauty, and artistry of the golf swing motion. We're fascinated by the impossible task of trying to roll a small ball across a perfectly manicured lawn and into a small hole in the ground. And the beauty of the surroundings and the camaraderie that is such a big part of the sport renews our spirits. Yes, we're hooked, and there is no cure. But we don't mind. We're simply nuts about golf.

19th Hole

DEAR HEAD NUT

Dear Sir,

I am a golf fanatic. Please send application for membership in the Golf Nuts Society. I play every weekend, including Christmas and my wedding anniversary, plus three evenings each week. That's five rounds a week, plus practice at lunchtime. Recently sold home to devote more time to golf.

Sincerely,
Kenneth Conrad
Lebanon, PA

Dear Head Nut,

I read with interest an article about your society. The typical member unfortunately describes my husband rather accurately. Golf is making a mess of everything around our house. Please send him a membership application to the address below. What about us golf widows? Do you have an auxiliary for those of us who gag at the word *golf*? Is there a club for children who have forgotten what their fathers look like because Dad lives at the golf course? Is there an available list of local mental health professionals that deal with family members to help them cope with this obsession? My husband does not know I have requested an application. It will come as a surprise to him. I can guarantee, however, that he will join.

If it says "golf" anywhere on the application, he must have it, join it, wear it, play it, use it, etc. Catch my drift?

Sincerely,
Mary Montero
Chesapeake, VA

Dear Golf Nuts Society,

Please let me know how I can join Golf Nuts. I was once hitting to a golf green that was slightly downhill with a small lake in front of the green. It took me seventeen shots to get over the water on to the green. I left the other sixteen balls in the water. Later that night I went back and waded into the water looking to find the balls, and wound up with 877 golf balls in less than one and a half hours. I am now a golf ball collector. I collect balls in the evenings, and sometimes I stay out as late as 5:00 in the morning. I now have more than 467,000 golf balls. I have more balls than anybody.

Sincerely,
Scott Deasy
Wynnewood, PA

Dear Sir,

I would like to apply for membership in the Golf Nuts Society. Enclosed is the application fee. My golf nut qualifications:

I had an appendectomy on a Monday – played golf on Thursday.

Two weeks before a scheduled golf trip to Wild Dunes, I dislocated my left ankle. My golf partners cut off the cast and I went on the trip. I played in one golf shoe and one moccasin.

Thank you,
Larry Levy
Millis, MA

Dear Golf Nuts Society,

Please send application for membership as soon as possible. I know I qualify. At one time I had thirty-three putters. The night before a golf outing I would line up all thirty-three, and about an hour later I would have selected five. The five that I selected, I would put under my mattress, and the one I dreamed about was the one that I would use in the tournament. That was twenty years ago, and now I only have two putters, but my wife of twenty-seven years still thinks I am a "golf nut."

Golfingly yours,
Kenneth C. Conrad
Centerline, MI

Dear Golf Nuts Society,

Please send me a membership application for my father. I was a golf orphan. I think he would fit in very well with the other whackos that belong to the Golf Nuts Society.

S. Jaffe
Hollywood, CA

Dear Mr. Nut,

I'm very interested in receiving two applications for membership. My golf partner, Paul, is a long-time sufferer. I only go with him six times a week so he'll feel better. This is really only for him. Myself, I'm a clinical psychologist in private practice, and have my life and game in proper balance. I hardly think that buying two sets of Ping irons, one set of Axioms, eight different combinations of metal woods, two Power Pods, and four different putters in the span of 120 days would qualify. I should, however, carry a bag tag so Paul wouldn't feel so bad. Thank you for understanding.

Fore always,
J.W. Baker III
Cedar Rapids, IA

Dear Head Nut,
   I'm enclosing a self-addressed stamped envelope. Please send me by return mail, application for membership in the Golf Nuts Society. I believe I have some of the necessary qualifications. I was playing golf in a snowstorm in Ithaca, NY on the day that my second son was born in Wisconsin.
                                                      Very truly yours,
                                                      R.E. Norene
                                                      Cedarburg, WI

Dear Head Nut,
   I appeal to you for a special ruling. On two separate occasions last week– once at 9:15 p.m., and once at 10:35 p.m. – I was asked by police to leave two golf courses because I was playing after hours (and after dark) with a Nitelite golf ball. Both times I was threatened with arrest on trespassing charges, but was released. I have been playing local courses at night for three months, have been caught seven times and arrested once. I would like a ruling on the special bonus point value of this unlawful, but delightful activity. I await your reply.
                                                      Always out-of-bounds,
                                                      Brian Turk
                                                      Phoenix, AZ

Dear Head Nut,
   I read with much interest and amusement the article in this week's *Sports Illustrated*. I, too, have played golf in a tornado (the one that wiped out Newton Falls, Ohio) and other weather that kept the nonlunatics off the golf courses. I hereby submit my application for membership to join your distinguished society. I would also request to be honorary chairman for Northeast Ohio (most certainly Hudson, Ohio.)
                                                      Hit 'em long & straight,
                                                      George W. Roth
                            Honorary Chairman-Elect for Northeast Ohio

Dear Head Nut,

On September 13th of this year, I was playing at Oswego Lake Country Club, and on the second hole I hit a good drive that struck a bird that was crossing the fairway. The bird died. I hit a 5-wood for my second shot about six feet from the hole. I putted the next shot in for a natural birdie. I got two birds on the same hole.

Thomas W. Crosswhite
Lake Oswego, OR
P.S. With my stroke on the hole, I got an eagle. That's three birds on the same hole!

Dear Head Nut,

I'm writing to you from the clubhouse because it's raining buckets on the course. I've been sitting here for two hours, waiting for it to quit. Anyway, I would like to join your club, and need to know where to sign up!

Truly nuts about golf,
Mark Wahlen
Bellvue, CO

Dear Sir,

I am not in a class with you guys! However, I have a story to tell of a "real nut." In 1977, while playing in Victoria, Vancouver Island, Canada, I was paired with an advertising/public relations executive from Seattle. On one of the par-3s, my ball almost went in for an ace. The gentleman asked me if I had ever had a hole-in-one. When I said "no," I returned the question. He said "yes," and that he had bought the portion of the green (one foot square), the cup, the flag, and the flagstick, and he has in his will that when he dies a special casket be made and all of the above be buried with him. I have been playing golf for 57 years, and that is the top of the line!

Sincerely,
Arthur G. Witters
Orlando, FL

Dear HN,

Even with all the wonderful high-tech ways of tracking each and every shot from each and every round, I still take great comfort in recording some notes and thoughts by hand. They make for hysterical reading about two seasons hence. Here's a stick-man drawing that I created during "the horror of '95," my worst year in golf.

Sincerely,

Bob "Captain Hook" Scavetta

Yonkers, NY

BALANCE!! FOCUS!! TEMPO!! BREATHE!! SLOWER!!

50% 75% ARC!! 100%

SWING EVERY IRON LIKE A WEDGE!

DON'T GET "HANDSY"

DON'T THROW IT FROM HERE!

THE GRIP!!
THE GRIP!!
SWING DOWN THEN AROUND!!

HAVE I WORKED ON THIS ZONE?

FULL SHOT ZONE -

NEVER PAST HERE!! →

POINTS AT TARGET →

TRUST THE SWING!

THINK! FOCUS! RELAX! SEE THE SHOT! POSITIVE GOLF THOUGHTS!

FIRE THE RIGHT SIDE

← BACK TO TARGET →

FLAT LEFT WRIST = STRAIGHT SHOT!

TURN!! DON'T SWAY!!

CONTROLLED AGGRESSION!

LESS IS MORE!

ALIGNMENT!

SOFT HANDS!

← TURN MIDDLE ½ AS FAR AS LEFT SHOULDER - TORQUE RESISTANCE!

BALL POSITION!

SWING PLANE! (SEE HOGAN)

← CLEAR THE HIPS!!

DON'T HOLD ON! DON'T PULL! ROTATE + RELEASE HANDS!

← DRIVE THROUGH WITH THE BIG MUSCLES -

STAY ON BALANCE!!

← KNEE FLEX -

SMOOTH! ONE MOVE!

← IMPACT ZONE KNEE TO KNEE →

FINISH THE SWING!

← DON'T JUMP AT IT!!

HOLD FINISH - HIGH HANDS!

← LEFT HEEL DOWN FOR CONTROL!

DRIVE DOWN + THROUGH!

← STANCE + FOOT ANGLES!

SWING THE CLUB!

TURN IN THE BARREL!

HAVE FUN!!

STAY BACK!

DON'T MAKE THE BALL THE TARGET - DRIVE THROUGH → COMPLETE THE CIRCLE!!

TEMPO!!

ONE PIECE TAKE AWAY!!

HINGE WRISTS NATURALLY!!

INTO A FIRM RIGHT SIDE

STAY DOWN!!

SWING

"1.5 SECONDS OF THOUGHT"

RS 1996

NUT NOTES

A Compendium of Completely Worthless and Useless Facts and Figures

---

GOLF NUTS SOCIETY FACT SHEET

FOUNDED: July 4, 1986
FOUNDER: Ron Garland, "The Head Nut"
BOARD OF DIRECTORS:
Ron Garland (#0001), Founder
Peter Moore (#0002), Former Creative Director, Nike, Inc. and adidas, Inc.
Michael Jordan (#0023), NBA Superstar
Bob Hope (#0025), The King of Comedy
Peter Jacobsen (#0022), PGA Tour Star
Gary McCord (#2274), CBS Golf Analyst & Senior PGA Tour Star
Marshall Holman (#0024), PBA Bowling Star
The Golfing Gorilla (#0565), World's Longest Hitting Gorilla
Chuck Hogan (#0611), World Renowned Golf Instructor
Bobby Rahal (#0026), Indianapolis 500 Winner
Dale Johnson (#0770), Retired Director of the Oregon Golf Association
Calvin Peete (#1142), PGA Tour Star
Kiki Vandeweghe (#1142), Former NBA Star
Amy Alcott (#0066), LPGA Tour Star
MOTTO: "If You're Not Registered, How Can You Be Committed?"
OFFICIAL GREETING: "Go Nuts!"
OFFICIAL FLOWER: *Poa Annua*
OFFICIAL BIRD: Eagle
OFFICIAL MOVIE: *Caddyshack*

OFFICIAL ALBUM: "Jake Trout & The Flounders"
OFFICIAL BOOK: *Golf Nuts – You've Got To Be Committed* by Ron Garland, with Brian Hewitt. Foreword by Michael Jordan.
PURPOSE: To Discover "The Secret."

CELEBRITIES
GOLF NUTS SOCIETY CELEBRITY MEMBERS

1.Michael Jordan (#0023) NBA Superstar
2.Bob Hope (#0025) The King of Comedy
3.Jack Lemmon (#0820) Oscar Award-Winning Actor
4.Peter Jacobsen (#0022) PGA Tour Star
5.Huey Lewis (#0819) Rock & Roll Star
6.Clint Eastwood (#1930) Oscar Award-Winning Actor
7.Neal Lancaster (#0029) PGA Tour Star
8.Lawrence Taylor (#2270) Former NFL All-Pro Linebacker
9.Bobby Rahal (#0026) Indianapolis 500 Winner
10.Julius Erving (#1497) Former NBA Superstar
11.Gary McCord (#2274) CBS Golf Analyst/Senior PGA Tour Star
12.Neil Lomax (#1265) Former NFL All-Pro Quarterback
13.John Havlicek (#1286) Former NBA Superstar
14.Peter Ueberroth (#1257) Former MLB Commissioner
15.The Golfing Gorilla (#0565) Golf Celebrity
16.Kiki Vandeweghe (#1142) Former NBA Star
17.Marshall Holman (#0024) 1988 PBA Bowler of the Year
18.Danny Ainge (#1264) Former NBA Star
19.Billy Olson (#1310) Former World Pole Vault Record Holder
20.Eddie Arcaro (#1608) Former Horseracing Jockey
21.Billy Cunningham (#1499) Former NBA Superstar
22.Roy Green (#2276) Former NFL All-Pro Wide Receiver
23.Amy Alcott (#0066) LPGA Superstar

24.Robert Trent Jones Jr. (#0731) Golf Course Architect
25.Chuck Hogan (#0611) World Renowned Golf Instructor
26.Dean Oliver (#0536) Rodeo Cowboy Hall of Fame
27.Dave Pelz (#1013) Founder of Pelz Golf Research ("Dr. Putt")
28.Calvin Peete (#1142) Senior PGA Tour Star
29.Shelby Futch (#2026) Founder, John Jacobs' Practical Golf Schools
30.Dan Majerle (#2372) NBA Star
31."Nellie" (#2709) Golf Nuts Society Director of Instruction

GOLF NUT RECORD BOOK
(Effective August 1, 2002)
OVERALL

All-Time Leading Scorer: Rob Gillette (#2374) – 63,688 Points
Entrance Examination Score: Ken Stankiewicz (#2858) – 18,813 Points
Bonus Points: Tom Jewell (#0175) – 48,419 Bonus Points

MECHANICS

Most Swing Changes (Single Competitive Round): The Head Nut (#0001)
- 6 ('87 Northwest Open)
Most Swing Changes (Single Noncompetitive Round): The Head Nut
(#0001) - 7
Most Swing Changes (Career): The Head Nut (#0001) - 3,847
Most Putting Stroke Changes (Single Competitive Round): Open
Most Putting Stroke Changes (Career): Open
Most Putter Changes (Single Year): Ronn Grove (#0830) - 54

CAPITAL ASSETS

Most Putters Purchased (Career): The Head Nut (#0001) - 154

Most Putters Purchased (Single Year): Jim Gibbons (#0394) - 7
Most Drivers Purchased (Career): Jim Jensen (#2730) - 150+
Most Drivers Purchased (Single Year): Al Jamieson (#1897) - 10
Most Expensive Driver Purchased: Jerry Lacey (#2022) - Maruman Suppan Tap, $1,700
Most Expensive Putter Purchased: The Head Nut (#0001) - Wilson "Designed by Arnold Palmer," $1,200
Most Sets of Irons Purchased (Single Year): Jerry Lacey (#2022) - 6
Most Sets of Irons: Todd Patch (#0119) - 9
Most Sets of Woods Currently Owned: Todd Patch (#0119) - 6
Most Golf Instruction Videos Purchased (Single Year): E.M. Vandeweghe (#1191) - 20
Most Golf Books Purchased (Single Year): Mike Wilkins (#2483) - 150
Most Logo Golf Towels: Tom Jewell (#0175) - 73
Most Logo Golf Shirts: Nobby Orens (#2259) - 292
Most Logo Golf Sweaters: Howie Smith (#0283) - 49
Most Logo Golf Caps: Greg Miles (#2681) - 113
Most Logo Golf Visors: Pat Seelig (#1627) - 75
Most Pairs of Golf Shoes: Howie Smith (#0283) - 34
Most Drivers: Jim Gibbons (#0394) - 25
Most Putters: Mike Noyes (#2211) - 135
Most Golf Clubs (All Types): Pat Seelig (#1627) - 250
Most Ball Markers: Boyd Sempel (#1085) - 24,000
Most Bag Tags: Jeffrey August (#1707) - 11,000
Most Logo Golf Balls: Greg Miles (#2681) - 8,341
Most Golf Books: Mike Noyes (#2211) - 2,259
Most Golf Videos: E.M. Vandeweghe (#1191) - 200
Most Golf Bags: Jim Gallagher (#2860) - 12
Most Scorecards: Pat Seelig (#1627) - 900
Most Golf Ties: Mike Noyes (#2211) - 98
Most Divot Repair Tools: Jane Minesinger (#1978) - 796

Least Expensive Country Club Dues: Ron Kulchak (#0532) - $20/year
Most Sets of Clubs Stolen from His Garage (Single Year): Joel Neilsen (#2703) - 4
Most Balls Hit Into His Yard in a Single Year by Bad Golfers: Jerry Kinder (#0480) -1,200

PERFORMANCE

Low Gross (GNS-Sanctioned Event): Warren Kovar (#1371) - 65
Low Net (GNS-Sanctioned Event): Chris Martin (#1127) - 64
High Gross (GNS-Sanctioned Event): Jeff Larsen (#0467) - 126
Longest Drive (GNS-Sanctioned Event): Joe Malay (#0020) - 340 Yards
Most Water Balls (GNS-Sanctioned Event): Jim White (#1138) - 16
Most OBs/LBs (GNS-Sanctioned Event): Norman Goldman (#0989) - 17
Most Penalty Strokes in a Winning Match: Joe "The Guru" Vieira (#2699) - 12
Most Putts (GNS-Sanctioned Event): Norman Goldman (#0989) - 42
Least Putts (GNS-Sanctioned Event): Jim Gibbons (#0394) - 25
Most States Played (Single Day): Scott Houston (#1186) - 7
Most States Played (Single Vacation): Merle Ball (#2040) - 50
Most States Played (Career): Merle Ball (#2040); Frank DeMore (#1019); Craig Fenton (#2308); Paul Pradia (#2309); Walt Lingo (#2307) - 50
Most Countries Played (Single Day): Nobby Orens (#2259); Mike Brands (#0774) - 2
Most Countries Played (Career): Bob Van Nest (#1975) - 54
Most Rounds Played (Single Vacation): Merle Ball (#2040) - 50
Most Golf Courses Played (Single Day): Scott Houston (#1186) - 7
Most Golf Courses Played (Career): Ed Gowan (#1982) - 1,467
Most "Top 100" Courses Played (Career): David Earl (#0615) - 39
Most PGA/LPGA/Sr. PGA Tour Events Attended (Single Year): Nellie (#2709) - 10

Most PGA/LPGA/Sr. PGA Tour Events Attended (Career): Todd Patch (#0119) - 67
Most Tour Pro's Played with (Career): Tom Jewell (#0175) - 135
Most "Holes-In-One" (Career): Jim Gallagher (#2860) - 4
Most Rounds Played (Single Year): Merle Ball (#2040) - 1,290
Most Rounds Played (Career): David Mikkelson (#0128) - 6,000
Most Tournaments Played (Single Year): Joe Malay (#0020) - 53
Most Tournaments Played (Career): Joe Malay (#0020) - 1,000 (and counting…)
Most Consecutive U.S. Opens Attended: Ron Morrow (#2852) - 19
Most Times Shot Your Age: Cy Perkins, lowest score was 65 (#0471) - 454 (as of 07/15/02)
Fastest 18-Hole Round: David N. Brown (#2893) - 29 min. 38.5 sec.
Most Balls Found on a Single Hole (While Playing): Ivan Morris (#2761) - 17

COMMITMENT

Lowest Temperature Round: Charles Gilmore (#0861) - (-40F degrees)
Cold Index Record: Tom Jewell (#0175) - -576 Index (20 degrees + -12 degrees wind chill x 18 holes)
Highest Temperature Round: Earl Kulson (#2005); Sandy Alexander (#2729) - 122F degrees
Heat Index Record (Cart): T.J. Futch (#2347) - 10,384 Index (118 Degrees x 88 Holes)
Heat Index Record (Walking): Sandy Alexander (#2729) – 2,196 Index (122 degrees x 18 holes)
Rainfall Index: Jeff Swartz (#2671) – 36 Index (2 inches x 18 holes)
Snow Index: Bob Spiwak (#2310) – 27 Index (3 inches x 9 holes)
Illness Index: Robert Koenigsberg (#0416) – 1,040 (10 holes x 104° body temperature)

Highest Wind Velocity: Bill Johnson (#0904) - 85 mph (Typhoon Condition 1)

Most Tornados (Career): T.H. Nut (#0001); George Roth (#0190) - 1 (both survived)

Most Times Struck by Lightning (Career): Open

Most Holes Played in a Single Day: Pete Schenk (#0007) - 280

Most Holes Played at Night: John Abendroth (#0250) - 12 (at PGA West!)

Most Holes Played With a Putter: Hendrik Sharples (#2882) - 18

Most Consecutive Hours Played without Stopping: Walt Chambers (#0286) - 31

Most Lessons Taken (Single Day): Nobby Orens (#2259) - 6

Most Lessons Given (Single Day): Nellie (#2709) - 343

Most Lessons Taken (Single Year): Open

Most Lessons Taken (Career): "High Tech Doc" Leinassar (#0009) - Hundreds

Most Times Late for Dinner (Single Year): The Head Nut (#0001) - 27

Most Times Late for Dinner (Career): The Head Nut (#0001) - 400+

Most Times Threatened with Divorce (Career): The Prez (#0003) - 52 Times/Year

Most Golf-Related Divorces (Career): The Prez (#0003); Tony Araquistain (#1261); Steve Thorwald (#0476) - 1

Most Children Named after a Golfer: Peter Shaerf (#2872) - 1 (Nicholas for Faldo)

Most Pets Named after a Golfer: Peter Shaerf (#2872) - 2 (Monty for Montgomerie; Ben for Hogan)

Most Ballmarks Fixed (Single Hole): Gary "Leeky" Jones (#2705) - 17

Most Ballmarks Fixed (Single Round): The Head Nut (#0001) - 50

Fastest 18-Hole Round (Riding in a Cart): Nobby Orens (#2259) - 90 minutes

Fastest 18-Hole Round (Walking): The Head Nut (#0001) - 1 hr. 50 minutes

Fastest 18-Hole Round (Running): David Brown (#2893) - 29 min. 38.5 sec.
Longest Distance Driven (Roundtrip) to Play a Single Round in a Single Day: Chris Veitch (#0151) - 870 miles
Longest Distance Flown (Roundtrip) to Play a Single Round in a Single Day: Nobby Orens (#2259) - 13,404 (Los Angeles to New Zealand to Los Angeles)
Longest Distance between Two Rounds in a Single Day: Nobby Orens (#2259) -13,404 (Los Angeles and New Zealand)
Longest Distance Hitchhiked to Play in a Tournament: Joe Malay (#0020) - 2,000 miles (from Weiser, Idaho to Johnstown, Pennsylvania)

MISCELLANEOUS

Most Incredible Ruling of All Time: Michael Jordan (#0023) - He was a "no-show" for his first NBA Most Valuable Player award. The NBA "brass" and the worldwide media were in Chicago for the presentation. He was playing 36 holes at Pinehurst with his buddies.2,000 Points
Most Points for a Single Ruling: Corbin Cherry (#2266)- Lost right leg below the knee in service to his country in Vietnam, but loved the game so much that he taught himself to play golf again wearing an artificial limb. Went on to qualify for both the 1995 USGA Senior Open and 1996 U.S. Senior Amateur, and played in both events, walking the entire way. 20,000 points
Best Excuse for Lousy Play (GNS-Sanctioned Event): Jeff Larsen (#0467) - Played in tournament with right arm in full-arm cast (shoulder-to-hand).1,000 points
Most Notable Achievement (GNS-Sanctioned Event): Dick London (#0988) - His wife went to Europe alone because he refused to miss the first annual GNS Championship. 1,000 points

THE GOLF NUT'S GLOSSARY

TEE SHOT

"He's more nervous than Woody Allen at a family reunion." – First tee jitters
"It felt like standing in Kuwait and having to hit one in the desert." – It
was a pretty wide fairway. *
"Take a suck a that!" – After you smoke one down the middle. *
*"I dialed up the big dog and stone pureed a screamin' pea that flew
everything."* – He hit a long drive over the dogleg.
"Then I hit one longer and straighter than I-80." – He hit a good drive.*
*"The skinny kid from _____ has really smacked that one, ladies and
gentlemen!"* – He hit a long tee shot.
*"The fat boy from _____ has really smacked that one, ladies and gen-
tlemen!"* – Ditto, except he isn't skinny.
"That one's out there where the big dogs piss." - That drive is long.
*"Did you hear they're building a new Wal-Mart? Really, where?
Between your drive and mine!"* – After you've just outdriven your oppo-
nent by fifty yards.
"Nice drive, this is a recording." – He has hit yet another fairway.

APPROACH SHOT

"It's time to shake some steel and rip some cloth." – He's planning to hit
it close today.*
"That shot was so pure that I never even heard it leave the clubface." –
He smacked it right in the sweet spot. *
*"It was loaded up with Tour cheese, just waiting to rip down some
cloth."* – It had some serious backspin on it, and it was headed for the flag.*
"I dead flat stacked it." – Hit it dead straight, right at the pin.
"I stiffed it." – Ditto

"I clotheslined it." – Ditto

"I roped it." – Ditto

"It inhaled the pin." – Ditto

"It was chewin' fiber!" - Ditto

"It did a jungle juice tango." – He spun that baby back.

"It landed soft as left-out butter." – It didn't roll very far after hitting the green. *

"It landed like a butterfly with sore feet." – Ditto

"I hit a little drop and stop wedge in there about three feet from the jar." – He checked his wedge shot in there three feet from the hole.

"TV golf!" – He stuck it close.

"Dead Solid Perfect" – A pretty good shot…and an even better book by Dan Jenkins.

"Right line, wrong ZIP code." – He just lasered an approach shot right over the flag and into the next county.

"Right club, wrong ZIP code." – He just hit his approach shot pin high, but about a hundred yards off line.

GOOD PUTT

"I put a stroke on my putt that was as pure as double cream." – It was a good stroke.*

"I just poured it in." – It was in all the way.

Jarred it. – Made the putt.

"I LOVE this game again!" – After making a short putt.

"Nice putt, this is a recording." – He has made yet another putt.

Pimp Walk – Strutting up to the hole like Jim Colbert after rolling in a snake.

BAD PUTT

"Think you used enough dynamite, there, Butch?" – He had a brain spasm and knocked it way past the hole. (*Butch Cassidy and the Sundance Kid*)
"I didn't even sniff the hole!" – Missed a short one.
"I three-whipped it." – He three-putted.
"I three-jacked" – Ditto
"I three-jerked it." – Ditto
"I three-whizzed all over myself." – Ditto
"A little chicken left on that bone, there Billy Bob." – He'll need to putt the comebacker.
"A little bit of pizza left in that box." – Ditto
"Did you get your putter caught in your skirt, dear?" – Left it short
Mick Jagger – A lip-out
Power Lip – A really good putt that somehow didn't stay in.
South American Putt - All it needed was one more revolution.

LONG PUTT

"I rolled in a seagoer to go 1-up." – Made a long one.
"I took her $20 with a 40-foot camel ride on the last hole." – Made a long one for the win. *
"It was so long that I needed a topo map just to find the hole." – It was a long putt.
"There were elephants buried out there!" – There were a few hills and valleys between him and the hole.
"It looked like they'd buried Mae West face up on my line!" – There were a couple of BIG hills between him and the hole.
Gag Lag – Came up a little short on a long one.
"He tanked one on sixteen that tore my heart out." – Made a long one

for the win. *
"Nuthin' but net!" – A dead-center putt.

SHORT PUTT

Throw up Zone – A three-footer.
The DMZ (Don't Miss Zone) – A three-footer (Compliments of Gary McCord)

GOOD PUTTER

"That's good." – What you say whenever a good putter hits the green.
"I can't stand to watch anymore." – He makes everything.
"Hey, Leon, can I buy your putter?" – What you say to someone who has just jarred a long one.
"The last time he missed one of those, I was still in grammar school." – After a good putter makes another short one.
Dudley Puttright – A disgustingly good putter *

BAD PUTTER

"You putt like Roberto Duran." – Hands of stone *

POOR PLAY

"I'm on my way to a serious radio station today. Magic 103." – Not exactly playing well. *
"He paid out like an ATM machine in spikes." – He wasn't very good. *
"See if they can give you a chili-dip vaccine while they're at it." – He's prone to chunking his chips. *
"We were a box of X-outs nobody wanted on the half-price table." –

They were a bunch of golf nuts who hung out at the local muni. *
"He had all his luck surgically removed as a small boy." – Luck was not
one of his strong points. *
Venturi – Overanalysis (as in, "Too much Venturi cost me a bogey back
on thirteen.") *

CHOKING

Takin' Gas
Leakin' Oil
Blew a Tire
The Wheels Came Off
Gagged
Suckin' Air
Tossed My Cookies
Swallowed the Apple
Tanked
  "I threw up all over my FootJoys on eighteen, and lost every ******
bet!"

SLOW PLAY

Class Reunion – More than one group on a tee.
"Those guys ought to pack a lunch!" – The group on the green is taking
a little too long on their putts.
"They're slower than refund checks." – Commenting on the group ahead.*
Captain Criscobutt – A very slow player
"I'm gonna have a birthday on this green!" – To a slow player in your
group.
"His doctor told him to take frequent naps during the day." – To one of
the foursome as a slow player is teeing off.

Four Siders - They look at every putt from all four sides.
The Dance of the Living Dead – A slow group up ahead.
Mall Walkers – They're in no particular hurry on the course.
Taxi!!- What you yell at a group in the fairway ahead, waiting to hit their shots to a green that none of them could reach unless they took a taxi.

FAST PLAYER

"Ready, Fire, Aim." – He's fast

ATTIRE

"He's found a custom fit in an off-the-rack world." – Good dresser *
"Now there's a fashion statement!" – His attire is not what you would call traditional.
"Did you pay money for that shirt?" - He is wearing an extremely ugly shirt.
"You're over the national logo limit." – There's one too many logos on your clothes. *
"Did you make it yourself?" – A backhanded compliment.
"I didn't know that purple and green went together" – A subtle hint.

GOOD SWING

"His swing is as smooth as a baby's behind." – He has a smooth swing.
"He paused at the top long enough to order a burger and fries." – He has good tempo.

BAD SWING

"What are you trying to do, win Hernia of the Month?" – After someone makes a particularly hideous swing. *

"Are you going to be okay?" - Ditto
"You swung so hard that you set your shoelaces on fire." – He has a very quick swing.*
"He had a Harley Davidson grip." – It was just a bit strong. *
"I gave it an industrial strength downward lurch." – It wasn't a very pretty swing. *
"Where'd you get that amphetamine phone booth swing?" – It was so quick, and so short that he could swing in a phone booth. *
"Okay, let's see that vitamin-deficient little swing of yours." – He doesn't exactly make a strong move at the ball. *

BAD HOLE

BIP – "Ball in pocket."
BIPSIC – "Ball in pocket, sit in cart."
DNFROB – "Did not finish, ran out of balls."

GOOD GOLFER

"He's been playing golf since he was old enough to chew solids." – He's experienced.*
"He hasn't been in the rough since Arnie was in diapers." – He hits it pretty straight.
"He can take it deep." – Long hitter
"He can take it low." – Can get it under par.
"He can go low." – Ditto

BAD GOLFER

Hack
Chop

GOOD SHOT

*"Boys, if you like golf, you **gotta** like that shot."* – He certainly liked it. *

"That's better than sex!" – He must be married.

"Do you think there's golf in heaven?" – He wants the feeling to last.

"God, I love this game." – He just hit a perfect shot.

Juice - Backspin

"I put some Michael Jackson on it." – He put some backspin (Moonwalk) on it.

"There was some serious "pro shit" on that one!" – Lots of backspin

"I had some cat scratch on it." - Ditto

"Chirp, chirp…" – Said after making a birdie.

"Tweet, tweet…" – Ditto

"Linda Ronstadt" – Blew by you! ("Blue Bayou")

"James Brown!" – "I Feel Good!" (…after that shot.)

Quail High – A low shot into the wind

"That baby will run like loose stool." – It should run for a while after it hits the ground.

"I just pureed that deuce out on fourteen." – He hit a pretty good 2-iron on the 14th hole.

"Suck on that, you muni hacks!" – He liked the shot. *

"It was so sweet, it brought tears to my eyes." – Ditto

TALKIN' TO YOUR BALL

"Be right!" – Be as good as you look!

"Be the number!" – Ditto

"Full Flaps!" – Come down, baby.

"Wheels up!" – Clear the trees!

"Run like a raped ape!" – Hit the ground running!

"Grow Teeth!" – Stop!

BAD SHOT

"The only thing that didn't move on that swing were my bowels." – He chunked it.

"I hit it into the worst lie since, "I did not have sex with that woman." – He didn't have a very good lie.

"I'm deader than a run-over dog." – He has hit it into a bad lie.

"I thought I was buried in the broccoli, but when I found that ball, it was sitting up like a hooker in a limousine!" – He hit into the rough, but drew a perfect lie.

"Oh no, the dreaded straight ball!" – He's hit one straight while playing for a slice.

"Then I started hitting some serious fishhooks." – He started hitting it left. *

"Welcome to the Jungle!" – He just snapped one off into the trees.

Eva Braun – A shot that went in the bunker

A Hoover – A shot that sucks *

Oscar Brown – Out-of-Bounds (OB)

Oscar Bonavena – Ditto

O'Brien - Ditto

Power Steering – "I put some power steering on that one. Had both hands on the wheel through impact."

Skank – A skulled shank

Breakfast Ball – A bad tee shot that earns a mulligan because you chose to have breakfast rather than warm up on the range.

The Sleeve Rule – Everyone gets to hit up to three tee balls on the first tee.

Dachshund Killer – A low ball *

"If patience was oil, I'd be about two quarts low right now." – He's had a series of very bad shots.

"The Golf Gods hate me." – After yet another bad shot or bad bounce.

BETTING

"Place your bets! Place your bets!" – On the first tee, in your best Rodney Dangerfield *Caddyshack* imitation, before anyone has teed off.
PWP – Either team may **P**ress **W**hen **P**issed.
IFP – Either team may invoke an In Flight Press any time that any ball is "in flight."
"Is that my friend in the rough, or is the asshole on the green?" – There's a serious money game going on between these two.
"He had me down, down, down, and out, so I gave him an "Aloha" on eighteen. – He was 1-down on three bets and had lost one, so he pressed all bets on the 18th tee.
"I must have my hearing aid turned down again." – When your opponent won't give you a short putt.
"You have such a nice stroke, I just enjoy watching it." – After your opponent asks you if his short putt is good.
"It's not bad." - Response when your opponent asks, "Is that good?" regarding his short putt.(Alternate response: "It's pretty good.")
"May The Force be with you." – Prior to your partner (or opponent) hitting a tough shot at a critical point in the match.
"Have you hit yet?" – To your opponent, after he sticks his approach close to the hole.
"Ninety percent of our team is 100% in trouble." – You have just hit a real bad shot.
"Are you on a nature tour, Bob?" – To your opponent as he hits yet another tee shot into the trees.
"I have every notion to jar this on your ass." – I'm gonna try real hard to make this putt. *
"No more Ernest & Julio, please." – Commenting on your opponent's excessive whining. *
"Never bet against genius." – After you make a lucky shot. *

"You should be in the Sandbag Hall of Fame." – They are world-class sandbaggers. *
"I will be pleased to accept absolutely free any complimentary presses from each and every one of you sorry hacks." – "You gonna press?" *
"Your ass is pressed." – "I press."

A TOUGH SHOT

Lottery shot – He has a one in a million chance of pulling it off.
"I had two chances on that shot, slim and none, and Slim is in Amarillo playin' poker." – It's an impossible shot.
"You'd better leave the headcover on for that one." – It's a very fast putt.
"That shot will require more patience than ambition." – It's a very difficult shot.

THE GOLF COURSE

The Playground – The course
The Lettuce – The rough
The Broccoli – Ditto
The Vegetables – Ditto *
The Freeway – The fairway
The Fast Lane – Ditto
"This place is to golf courses what Spam is to the great chefs of Europe." – Not exactly in the U.S. Open rotation. *

PRACTICING

The Rockpile – The driving range
The Lab – Ditto
The Office – Ditto

Ammo – Range balls
Bunsen Burner – Video camera

GOLF CLUBS

Bats – Clubs (as in, "I don't think Hoover's gettin' along with his new bats.") *
Sticks - Ditto
Toys – Ditto
Weapons – Ditto
Tools - Ditto

TYPES OF GOLFERS

Range Rat – Likes to hit balls
Sandbagger – Likes an edge, and will massage his handicap to get it.
Turtle – Slow player
Numeral – Winner of the gene pool lottery. Trust fund baby. Member of the "Lucky Sperm Club."*
Mr. Goodgolf – A good player
Grinder – Has absolutely no game, but always finds a way to shoot a number.
Clubhouse Lawyer – A master of the handicap and the Rules of Golf
High-Tech Warrior – He has all the latest equipment.
Dead Man Walking – He said he'd be home at noon, but he decided to play another eighteen.

RABBIT EARS

"He could hear a mouse pissin' in a cotton field."
"He could hear the sailboats out on the lake."

Hit and Whip – Blaming a fellow player for a bad swing. *

TEMPER TANTRUMS

"Get the net!" – He's turned into a wild, rabid animal after hitting a bad shot.
"He went triple certifiable." – He went nuts. *
"He went double O.J. out on fourteen." - Ditto

CADDIE TALK

"It's the full value of the club, sir." – Caddie responding to the question, "Should I hit a full 8-iron?"
"Give me your best Arnie pose on this one." – Caddie's final admonishment before golfer hits the shot.
"Right out of the factory, baby." – This is the perfect club for this shot.

COURSE CONDITIONS

"We had a big Seeger goin' out there today." - It was blowin'.
"Noah and his ark floated by out on seven." – It was raining pretty hard.
"It was so cold that my teeth hurt!" – It was cold.

MISCELLANEOUS

"That'll require an environmental impact study!" – A very deep divot.
Emergency Nine – Another nine holes after the Saturday morning eighteen.
"Geez, I think I'd rather have cancer!" – Responding to someone who tells you he has the shanks.
Full Harley – A strong grip.

All glossary terms with asterisks printed with permission from the classic golf novel Missing Links, *by Rick Reilly*

GOLF NUT QUIZ
How Nuts Are You?

Here's a 20-question sampler from the infamous Golf Nuts Society Entrance Exam that will tell you how nuts you are.

SECTION I
COMMITMENT

1. I have played golf in the rain, snow, sleet, hail, hurricane, tornado, typhoon, thunderstorm, or earthquake during my career. *(100 points each)*
    Bonus: Was struck by lightning while playing, but finished the round.

2. I have played golf on:
    New Year's Day: *100*
    Easter *100*
    Mother's Day (Men) / Father's Day (Women) *200*
    Thanksgiving *100*
    Christmas *200*
    Spouse's Birthday *100*
    Bonus: Achieved "Golf Nut Slam" by playing in all of above in a single year. *1,000*

3. I've been threatened with divorce over golf at least once during my career. *100*

4. I've played "hooky" from work to play golf. *100*
    Bonus: Got caught by my boss. *100*
    Bonus: Got fired. *200*

5. I have quit the game forever___times in my career. *(10 points/time 500 points max)*
    Bonus: Sold my clubs. *100*
    Bonus: Threw clubs, bag, shoes, and cap into nearest lake. *150*
    Bonus: Retrieved them the next day. *200*

SECTION II
ATTITUDE

1. I say, "I hate this game!" after a bad shot at least once during almost every round. *50*
    Bonus: But it takes just one good shot for me to say, "I love this game!" *50*

2. When asked, "What did you shoot today?", I always answer, "I shot___, but it should have been____." *100*
    Bonus: I always recount my round, shot by shot, to some poor, unsuspecting victim such as spouse, children, playing companions, or bartender. *50*

3. If confronted with the accusation that "You love golf more than me, I answer:
    A. "Of course I do." *200*
    B. "But I love you more than tennis." *50*

4. When faced with the decision to play golf or watch it on television, I would:
    A. Watch golf on television *25*
    B. Play golf *50*
    C. Play golf and tape the telecast *100*

5.   I have____shirts, caps, visors, sweaters, skirts, shorts, or socks with a golf logo *(10 points/logo - 1,000 points max)*

SECTION III
MECHANICS

1.   I would describe my golf swing as:
     A. Modern *25*
     B. Classic *50*
     C. Antique *100*
     D. Neanderthal *200*

2.   I have taken____lessons from my pro during my career.
     (10 points/lesson - 500 points max)
     Bonus: My pro won't give me lessons. *100*
     Bonus: I've attended at least one golf school during my career. *200*
     Bonus: They gave me a refund and sent me home. *500*

3.   I have filmed my swing____times. *(25 points/time - 500 max)*
     Bonus: Got sick watching the film. *100*

4.   I check my swing in a mirror or picture window at least once each day. *100*
     Bonus: I was off plane as usual. *50*

5.   I practice my swing in the living room in the evenings:
     A. At least once a week. *25*
     B. Every night *100*
     Bonus: Put a dent in the coffee table *100*
     Bonus: Took a divot out of the carpet *100*

6. I have bought at least one high-tech, fuel-injected, turbo-charged driver. *100*
   Bonus: Couldn't hit it. *50*

7. I occasionally practice before work. *50*
   Bonus: I get up earlier for golf on the weekend than I do for work. *100*

8. I talk to my ball after I hit it ("Bite!," "Sit!," "Get up!," "Get down!") *50*
   Bonus: It never listens. *100*

9. Said, "I've got it!" while warming up on the practice range. *25*
   Bonus: "Lost it" on the way to the first tee. *25*
   Bonus: "Found it" again on the last swing of the day. *25*

10. I've discovered "THE SECRET" so many times during my golf career that I've lost track of the number!(This game is going to drive me nuts! What time do we play tomorrow?) *500*

TOTAL NUT POINTS_____

CONGRATULATIONS! You've completed the Golf Nut Quiz, a sampling of 20 questions from the infamous Golf Nuts Society Entrance Exam. How nuts are you? If you scored under 500 Nut Points, you need to *get* committed. If you scored over 1,000 Nut Points, you need to *be* committed! In either case, be sure to call 1-800-GOLFNUT to become a Registered Golf Nut, and learn how you can become a Lifetime Member!

HOW NUTS ARE YOU?
GET COMMITTED TODAY!

JOIN THE GOLF NUTS SOCIETY

Here are just a few of the benefits of membership:

- Official Bag Tag
- Membership Card with Your Own Personal Nut #
- Our Infamous Entrance Exam
- Weekly Golf Nuts News e-Newsletter
- Regular e-mails from The Head Nut (Nut Case of the Week, Golf Nut Record book, Dear Head Nut email of the Week, Nutflash Bulletins, etc.)
- Automatic Entry into the Annual Golf Nut of the Year Competition
- Invitation to the Annual Golf Nuts Championship
- Golf Nut Getaways to Unique and Interesting Golf Destinations
- Golf Nuts Golf Schools
- Discounts on Golf Equipment, Accessories, Training Aids, Unique Golf Gifts, and more!
- Free Online Golf Lessons from "Nellie," the Golf Nuts Society's Director of Instruction
- Access to "Members Only" Areas of Our Official Website (GolfNuts.com)
- Access to the Golf Nuts Network, where you can "hook" up with other members for golf anywhere in the world.

Join the fun and become part of the most unique golf association in the world!

TO JOIN

Call 1-800-GOLFNUT (465-3688)
or...
Go to www.GolfNuts.com and click on "Join Today!"

Don't Bogey This One!

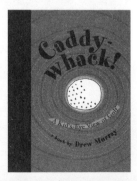

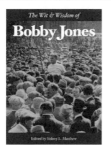

The Wit & Wisdom of Bobby Jones

By Sidney L. Matthew, Foreword By Bob Jones IV
Retail Price: $14.95
Sportsmen continue to marvel that Bobby Jones's legacy remains unparalleled in golf history. One of the reasons why is because Jones was more than the consummate champion golfer. This collection of quotes captures his spirit.

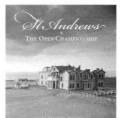

St. Andrews & The Open Championship: The Official History

By David Joy and Iain Macfarlane Lowe
Retail Price: $45
When one thinks of the Open Championship (British Open), it's hard not to think of the Old Course at St. Andrews as well. And no wonder. The Open Championship was first played at St. Andrews in 1873. Since then, the Open has returned to St. Andrews again and again. Each time, the game has been better for it.

Lost Links: Forgotten Treasures of Golf's Golden Age

By Daniel Wexler
Retail Price: $45
Literally hundreds of classic courses from golf's pre-World War II Golden Age have vanished over the years, including nearly 200 courses designed by legendary architects like Donald Ross, A.W. Tillinghast and Dr. Alister MacKenzie. This book includes 70 of the very best bygone courses and holes in America.